The Tontine: A History

From the last decades of the seventeenth century until the beginning of the twentieth, the tontine, in one form or another, was a ubiquitous financial instrument. As a revenue-raising tool of governments it supported the cost of war, and as a private capital-raising instrument it provided funding for civic improvement and urban development projects.

While the tontine is known today mainly through fictional works (Robert Louis Stevenson, Agatha Christie, and The Simpsons among others), this book tells the history of how it evolved from a public revenue-raising scheme into a popular private investment and infrastructure financing tool, before it was displaced by cheaper forms of borrowing. Focusing on the early development of the tontine, and with European and North American case studies, the narrative brings to life the story of a little-understood financial innovation.

This concise and engaging book is an ideal introduction to the history of the tontine for all readers interested in financial history.

Andrew McDiarmid earned his PhD from the University of Dundee and attended Yale University's Graduate School of Arts and Sciences. His research focuses on financial history from the early modern period to the twentieth century, with his first monograph on the subject of the Scottish Financial Revolution released in 2023. He is currently the SFI/IRC pathways fellow at University College Dublin, where he is undertaking a major project exploring the history of tontines between the seventeenth and nineteenth centuries.

Routledge Focus on Financial History

About the Series

'Routledge Focus on Financial History' is a series of short form (20,000-50,000 words), accessible books telling the origin stories behind financial instruments, innovations and institutions. Each book provides historical context on the early development of topics such as investments, money, insurance, banking, central banks and financial theory. The emphasis is on engaging storytelling and clarity, making these topics interesting and understandable to a non-specialist audience.

The Tontine: A History

Andrew McDiarmid

Routledge
Taylor & Francis Group
LONDON AND NEW YORK

First published 2025
by Routledge
4 Park Square, Milton Park, Abingdon, Oxon OX14 4RN

and by Routledge
605 Third Avenue, New York, NY 10158

Routledge is an imprint of the Taylor & Francis Group, an informa business

British Library Cataloguing-in-Publication Data
A catalogue record for this book is available from the British Library

ISBN: 9781032791999 (hbk)
ISBN: 9781032792064 (pbk)
ISBN: 9781003491002 (ebk)

DOI: 10.4324/9781003491002

Typeset in Times New Roman
by codeMantra

For Lorenzo.
From one chancer to another.

Contents

Acknowledgements

As there are several buildings in Scotland that retain the word 'tontine' in their name, it is likely that I was aware of the term on some level, but as I read P.G.M. Dickson's work on the Financial Revolution in England, there it was.[1] Dickson suggested that William Paterson, a Scotsman who was instrumental in setting up the Bank of England and was responsible for the plan to establish a Scottish colony in Darien, was also behind the first English tontine of 1693. As I read this in late 2017, I was approaching the end of my doctoral research and working towards the completion of my thesis on the Scottish Financial Revolution, in which Paterson was an important figure. An English tontine wasn't really of interest to me then, and I likely looked up the meaning for context and moved on.

As I read Dickson's work, I was attending Yale's Graduate School of Arts and Sciences. To acclimatise to my new surroundings, I visited the New Haven Museum. There, I was met by a photo of the now long defunct Tontine Hotel, which had previously stood in the city. Seeing the word again made me take notice. Then, shortly after that, as I searched the catalogue of Yale's Beinecke Library for unrelated material, the tontine again appeared. The synchronicity of this word appearing multiple times piqued my interest. Fortunately, just two years earlier in 2015, Moshe Milevsky had released his excellent work on the English tontine of 1693. There are not many academic books that could be described as 'page turners', but Moshe's prose drew me in, and between that and the rather macabre concept of the tontine itself, I was hooked.

Since late 2018 I have put a lot of hours into the tontine, scouring academic and non-academic works, local and national archives at home and abroad, and newspapers, for any mention of the scheme. Like any historical research, the topic could be elusive. For the tontine this often meant a reference to it in a letter or a newspaper, but with little more information. Or it involved finding a prospectus for a scheme, before the trail ultimately went cold. Despite these challenges, each fragment of information uncovered provided an insight into the way tontines were historically used, gradually piecing together a fuller picture of the scheme's importance.

While at times it has been a frustrating process, overall, it has been an illuminating journey. Coming to understand the extent to which the tontine impacted the spaces and the culture of our towns and cities in the past has been a fascinating revelation. It is hoped that this book conveys the scope of this impact to the reader.

My gratitude goes to Moshe Milevsky for his work, his support, and his friendship. Thank you to Ivar McGrath, his support, along with that of the wider History department at University College Dublin, has been invaluable. Thank you also to Carl Wennerlind for his advice and support. And thank you to my editor at Routledge, Andy Humphries, for being so enthusiastic about this book and the series it is a part of.

I am thankful to the Irish Research Council (IRC) and Science Foundation Ireland (SFI), with the research herein supported in part by funding from the IRC and SFI under the Pathway grant 22/PATH-A/10618. Thank you also to the Royal Society of Edinburgh (RSE) for their support during 2022, with sections of the work which underpins this book being carried out under the RSE Saltire Early Career Fellowship award.

Lastly, thank you to Hugh for answering the phone every time I call. Thank you to Statia for looking after me. Thank you as always to my mum and dad. And thank you to Colette for everything.

Note

1 P.G.M. Dickson, *The Financial Revolution in England: A Study in the Development of Public Credit, 1688–1756* (London: Routledge, 1993)

A Note on Money and Inflation

Between the mid-seventeenth and the twentieth centuries, traditional tontines could be found across Europe and North America. As such, tontine subscriptions were historically paid for in various currencies. To give the reader a sense of the sums raised via different tontines, a list of the currencies mentioned in this book and their approximate exchange rate into sterling has been provided. Work by German academic, Georg Heinrich Paritius, on contemporary exchange rates has been hugely helpful in this process.[1] Paritius' figures are, however, limited to the years 1707 to 1709, and therefore do not account for exchange rate fluctuations throughout the entire period covered in this book. In spite of this limitation, by providing these early eighteenth-century conversion rates the reader will be better placed to understand the size and scope of historic tontines.

While Paritius' work has done much of the heavy lifting on exchange rates, there remains a real difficulty in determining modern currency values. Priced at £100 each, a subscription to English and British government tontines was a large amount of money, but exactly how large is a complex question. The Bank of England inflation calculator values £100 in 1709 at around £15,000 in 2024.[2] The bank is very open in stating, however, that this is only a 'rough guide', and that 'comparisons of prices further back in time and over long periods are less accurate than comparisons over short periods in recent years'.[3] The figure of £15,000 could therefore be wildly inaccurate, with just a slight increase in inflation rate growing the modern-day equivalent of £100 dramatically.

For example, using continuous compounding (where interest is calculated and added to the principal sum continuously) to get to £15,000 in 2024 from £100 in 1709, requires an average of 1.6 per cent inflation over the term of 315 years.[4] If this was increased by just one per cent, to 2.6 per cent, this would increase the value of £100 in 1709 to around £350,000 today.[5] A far better way of illustrating the vast sums which were being invested in historic tontines is to ask what did it take to earn £100 at the start of the eighteenth century when compared to today?

As Adam Smith stated in 1776, '[t]he real price of every thing, what every thing really costs to the man who wants to acquire it, is the toil and trouble of acquiring it'.[6] As is the case today, wages varied greatly across different forms of employment in the early eighteenth century. In 1710, an agricultural labourer could expect to earn around £17 per year, while a skilled worker, such as a shipbuilder, had an average salary of around £40.[7] Those working as 'police, guards, [and] watchmen', received £13 a year, while engineers and surveyors collected £131 over the same period.[8] This means that for the most poorly paid, £100 was around seven and a half years' salary, while even for high earners it represented most of their annual pay.

Thankfully today, while inequalities still exist, there have been legal provisions around pay designed to protect workers. In 2024, the UK National Living Wage was set at £11.44 an hour for workers over the age of twenty-one, allowing an unskilled labourer working 40 hours per week to earn £23,795 per annum before tax. If we consider someone working in this role in 1710, earning £17 per year, this means that £100 at that time was equal to 5.88 years' salary. Applying this calculation to a 2024 unskilled laborer's salary (£23,795 x 5.88), we can estimate that £100 in 1710 held equivalent value for this class of worker as approximately £140,000 does for their modern counterparts.

Admittedly this is not an exact science, wages have increased through legislative changes, not just through inflation. It is hoped, however, that this calculation conveys to the reader the real historical value of £100, and provides an understanding that this was a significant amount of money. For even if we accept the Bank of England's conservative calculation, paying £15,000 for one share in an investment is a significant amount of money, never mind the potential £350,000. By calculating this in terms of wages it provides us with a median figure which best expresses the value of £100.

The Currencies

Danish Rigsdaler

Paritius did not provide a value for the Danish rigsdaler, but he did for the Swedish riksdaler; a coin which was priced similarly to the Danish coin.[9] In 1709 he valued 40 of the Swedish coin at £9. £100 sterling was therefore equivalent to approximately 445 Swedish riksdaler in that year, with the Danish rigsdaler at a similar value.

Dutch Guilder

In 1709, Paritius valued 100 guilders at £9. £100 sterling was therefore equivalent to around 1,112 Dutch guilders in that same year.

Italian Lira

The various regions which make up modern-day Italy did not begin the process of unification until 1861. Prior to this, coinage was decentralised, with various regions issuing their own lira. As an example, Paritius valued the 100 Venetian lire at £3 in 1709, thus making £100 equivalent to approximately 3,334 Venetian lire in the same year.

Irish Pound

By the 1770s the Irish Pound traded almost at parity with the pound sterling.[10]

French Livre

In 1709, Paritius valued 40 livres at £3. £100 sterling would therefore have been the equivalent of around 1,334 livres at that time.This changed, however, leveling out to an exchange rate of 24 to 1 across the eighteenth century, increasing £100 to around 2,400 livres on average.[11]

'German' Florins

The tontines discussed in this book which operated in German and German-speaking territories did so before the process of German unification began in the second half of the nineteenth century. Prior to this, moves towards a unified currency had begun in the 1830s.[12] This fixed 24.5 florins of thc south German states as being equivalent to the Cologne mark, a unit of weight which was important to currency standards across the area. While Paritius did not provide details on the florin, it is known from elsewhere that 1 thaler was equivalent to 1.75 florins.[13] As Paritius valued 40 thalers from the Holy Roman Empire at £9 in 1709, this means that 70 florins (40 x 1.75) was also equivalent to £9. £100 sterling was therefore valued at around 778 florins in 1709.

'German' Thalers

The thaler was used extensively across German and German-speaking territories with those produced in different regions varying in value. As stated above, 40 thalers originating from the Holy Roman Empire were valued at £9 in 1709. £100 sterling was therefore equivalent to around 444 thalers in that year.

US Dollar

While deviating grossly during times of war, the US dollar averaged around $5 to £1 Sterling throughout the eighteenth century.[14] £100 sterling was therefore worth around $500 during this time.

Currency	*Approximate conversion to £100 in Year*
Danish Rigsdaler	445 in 1709
Dutch Guilder	1,112 in 1709
Venetian Lira	3,334 in 1709
Irish Pound	100 in 1773
French Livre	1,334 in 1707
'German' Florins	778 in 1709
'German' Thalers	445 thalers in 1709
US Dollar	500 on average during the eighteenth century

Notes

1 G.H. Paritius, *Cambio Mercatorio,* (Regensberg: n.p., 1709); a very helpful website which uses Paritius' figures and provides calculation tools can be found at http://www.pierre-marteau.com/editions/1709-cambio-mercatorio.html#reg

2 This year has been chosen as it aligns with Paritius' currency exchanges.

3 All figures are correct as of June 2024.

4 This assumes that interest (in this case inflation) is compounded and added back into the balance indefinitely (although in this case for 315 years).

5 Thank you to Moshe Milevsky for his discussion on this topic and his explanation of the calculations involved.

6 A. Smith, *An Enquiry into the Nature and Caus*es of *the Wealth of Nations*, Book 1, Chapter 5 (London: T. Nelson, 1852), pp.12–13.

7 Figures taken from J.G. Williamson, 'The Structure of Pay in Britain, 1710–1911', *Research in Economic History*, Vol. 7 (1982), pp.1–54.

8 J.G. Williamson, 'The Structure of Pay in Britain, 1710–1911', *Research in Economic History*, Vol. 7 (Greenwich, Conn: JAI Press, 1982).

9 J. Tarkka, 'The North European Model of Early Central Banking', in D. Mayes and G. Wood (eds), *Designing Central Banks* (Abingdon: Routledge 2009), p.42.

10 Y. Li and C. Rothschild, 'Adverse Selection and Redistribution in the Irish Tontines of 1773, 1775, and 1777', *Journal of Risk & Insurance, The American Risk and Insurance Association*, Vol. 87, No. 3 (2020), fn1. p.723.

12 M. Milevsky, *King William's Tontine: Why the Retirement Annuity of the Future Should Resemble Its Past* (Cambridge, 2015), p.97.

12 L. Einaudi, *Money and Politics: European Monetary Unification and the International Gold Standard (1865–1873)* (Oxford: Oxford University Press, 2001), p.35.

13 L. Einaudi, *Money and Politics: European Monetary Unification and the International Gold Standard (1865–1873)* (Oxford: Oxford University Press, 2001).

14 L.H. Officer and S.H. Williamson, 'Computing "Real Value" Over Time with a Conversion Between U.K. Pounds and U.S. Dollars, 1791 to Present', *MeasuringWorth*, 2024. Available at https://www.measuringworth.com/calculators/exchange/

1 The Tontine

Here, There, and Everywhere

When it comes to money, if something appears too good to be true, it probably is. But there are anomalies. One such case was the French tontine subscriber who received an incredible return on their initial stake. The lucky investor, Charlotte Barbier, a 59-year-old Parisienne, purchased a 300 livres share in the inaugural French government tontine of 1689 and was named as the tontine nominee.[1] Seven years later, in 1696, she enrolled in the second French tontine for the same sum and was again named as nominee. In exchange for the price of her shares, Barbier was guaranteed an annuity of at least 10 per cent (60 livres) for the rest of her life.[2] The tontine principle is, however, one which rewards survivorship, and as the mortality rate among the nominee pool in both tontines increased, so too did subscriber annuities. Barbier's annuity grew year on year, until she was the last surviving nominee in her class in both tontines.[3] By the time of her death in 1726, at the age of 96, she was in receipt of 73,500 livres per year from the tontines; a figure well in excess of €1 million today.[4] This astonishing amount equated to a 12,000 per cent return but is made all the more staggering by the fact that this was for just one year, the last of Barbier's life. For the 36 years prior to this, she had been in receipt of a steadily increasing annuity. The full realised return when compared to the initial outlay, was therefore truly phenomenal.

This story is likely one which will divide the readership. Some may be thinking, 'this tontine stuff sounds great, where can I sign up?' While others, despite Madame Barbier's excellent return, may have *a priori* knowledge of the tontine and would rather just steer clear of it altogether. For those of you in the first group, beware, for historic tontines were not always a lucrative investment. As we will see in Chapters 2 and 5, there were enough complaints from subscribers to large-scale public tontines and holders of tontine life insurance policies about low rates of return to confirm that the experience detailed above was not typical. For those of you in the second camp, this is an understandable view, for the tontine is a financial instrument with a bad reputation. This has largely been fuelled by literary representations of the scheme, which since the eighteenth century have perpetuated a narrative in which tontine subscribers were so incentivised by greed that they were prepared to

DOI: 10.4324/9781003491002-1

commit any number of immoral acts in order to increase their profits.[5] The literary connection between crime and the tontine then became more extreme from the turn of the twentieth century onwards, as writers of detective stories and murder mysteries, both in literature and on screen, often used the tontine as a motive for murder.[6] These stories pushed the realities of the tontine. For while there were undoubtedly instances of fraud linked to the scheme, there is no evidence that a murder was ever motivated by a tontine.[7] Still, for many of us there is something about benefiting from the deaths of others which sends our moral compasses into a spin whether it is legal or not.

The Tontine Principle

So, what exactly was this scheme that offered the chance of truly exceptional returns, and which drove some of its participants to engage in criminality?[8] In its simplest historical form, the tontine was a scheme which provided investors with a yearly payment (annuity) in exchange for a one-off initial payment. At the outset anyone buying a tontine share (the subscriber) was required to name an individual (the nominee) against whose life the share was secured. The nominee could be anyone the subscriber chose. They might select themselves or another family member, or occasionally a public figure, such as a young royal, was chosen.[9] When payment became due, usually at the end of the first year of the tontine, the subscriber received their first annuity payment, and continued to do so, year on year, for as long as their nominee remained alive.

So far, this sounds very much like a regular life annuity, but where things become interesting, rather macabrely, is when nominees started to die. When this happened and the associated subscriber was no longer entitled to their annuity, this sum was redistributed between those subscribers who still had a living nominee. This meant that the rate of the annuity for active subscribers increased and continued to do as more nominees died; this is exactly what happened with the Parisienne investor. It was therefore possible, unless a tontine was organised in such a way to prevent it from happening, that the subscriber with the last living nominee would collect an annuity to the amount that had previously been divided among every other subscriber in the tontine.[10]

A Quick Maths Lesson

An example of how the tontine principle works:

- If a tontine organiser sold 100 shares in their scheme with each priced at £100, this would raise a total of £10,000
- In exchange for the price of the share each subscriber is guaranteed an initial annuity paid at 5 per cent interest (this is just an example, with rates of interest changing from scheme to scheme)

- Five per cent of the total £10,000 is £500, so the annuity pot is fixed at £500 per year
- This means that when the scheme commences and all 100 nominees are alive, each subscriber will receive an annuity of £5 (£500/100 = £5)

The important point to understand is that the annuity pot is fixed, this never changes. How it is divided is the factor that changes.

- For example; if 25 nominees die, then the £500 dividend pot would be split between the surviving 75, giving each subscriber an annuity of around £6.66 (500/75 = 6.66)
- When half of the nominee pool has died, the remaining 50 subscribers would receive an annuity of £10 (£500/50 = 10)
- And when one subscriber remains, they would be the beneficiary of the full annuity of £500 per year until their nominee died

This is a very simple way to structure a tontine, but it is this correlation between increasing nominee mortality and increasing payments for survivors that defines the tontine principle.

Who, What, When, Where, and Why

Between the mid-seventeenth and the early twentieth centuries various forms of tontine were used by public and private groups across large sections of the globe. These included numerous regions of continental Europe, Britain and Ireland, Canada, the United States, and the Caribbean. The tontine concept also existed as an insurance tool in Russia, and the word 'tontine' is presently applied to a range of financial schemes in Africa and Asia; these are, however, savings, credit, and peer-to-peer lending tools, rather than traditional tontines, and do not have the benefit of survivorship.[11]

As we will cover in Chapter 2, the tontine had a murky conception. The scheme took its name from Lorenzo de Tonti, an equally murky Italian often mistakenly cited as a Neapolitan banker and one-time governor of the city of Gaeta, who proposed the tontine to the French government in 1652. The crown responded favorably to the idea, printing a series of royal orders which endorsed the tontine. Yet, despite this, several concerns raised by the *Parlement de Paris*, led to the plan being shelved at this time.

In the following decades, tontines emerged in Denmark, German-speaking territories, and the Dutch Republic. Then in 1689, the French government revived Tonti's original proposal and issued the first large-scale government tontine. The English followed suit in 1693, with the Irish government getting in on the act during the 1770s. Between 1689 and 1789, these three governments collectively offered 17 tontines, typically issuing them during times of war.

These represented the largest examples of public tontines ever offered and raised millions for their respective governments.[12] They also drew a great amount of interest from the public and from important thinkers of the period. Astronomer Edmund Halley, for example, produced life tables which coincided with the first English tontine of 1693, and possibly acted as an adviser to tontine investors. While later, in 1776, at the time of the Irish schemes, moral philosopher and political economist, Adam Smith shared his view that the tontine 'generally [sold] for something more than it is worth' due to 'the confidence which every man naturally has in his own good fortune'.[13]

During the second half of the eighteenth century, as cheaper forms of the government borrowing developed, the tontine's shine began to wear off. As a result the last large public tontine was issued in 1789 by the British government. Concurrent with this, however, was the uptake of the scheme among private groups across Europe and North America to fund civic improvement and urban development projects. This saw small local tontines established, with funds directed at the costs of building hotels, coffeehouses, churches, and any number of other projects. Annuities were then paid from rents or profits, and in many cases the last subscriber took ownership of the building itself.[14] The scheme was also used by private groups as an investment tool, whereby the tontine fund was invested in some form of stock, and annuities were paid from stock dividends. These private tontines proved to have a long shelf life, with the earliest active scheme being identified in the 1750s and the last in the 1870s.[15]

Throughout the nineteenth century tontine development went in several directions. As well as the continuation of the private schemes outlined in the last paragraph, there was the emergence of a mutual aid model of tontine from the 1830s onwards. Particularly prevalent in Ireland and the Merseyside area of England, these were small, local schemes which provided subscribers with a defined benefit, usually sickness and burial cover or access to a benevolent fund, in exchange for a weekly subscription. The tontine function of the scheme was then derived from the practice of dividing any monies remaining in the fund among surviving subscribers each Christmas.[16]

Meanwhile across the Atlantic, the tontine was incorporated into a novel form of life insurance in the United States. Developed by the Equitable Life Assurance Society in the late 1860s, tontine life insurance policies combined aspects of the tontine principle with life insurance. These required policyholders to forgo annual dividends for a 'tontine period' ranging from 5 to 20 years, in exchange for an eventual annuity comprised of the deferred dividends, accumulated interest, and a share of forfeited funds from policies terminated by either death or a lapse of payment during the tontine period. These appealed to the gambling instincts of investors and initially proved to be incredibly popular. This was until complaints over low returns, along with a lack of transparency and proper accounting, brought several investigations into the instrument. As a result of the legal reforms which followed, tontine life insurance policies were effectively outlawed in the United States by 1910.

While small mutual aid tontines continued to exist in Britain and Ireland, their use declined significantly during the first half of the twentieth century. This decline, coupled with the ban tontine life insurance in the United States, marked the end of any substantial applications of the tontine principle in the Western world for the remainder of the century.

The Aim of This Book

This scope of this book is to provide a concise history of the tontine. Think of it as part origin story and part greatest hits. This means it will not cover every historical tontine; this would likely not be desirable or of interest to the reader and would quickly become obsolete as more tontines are uncovered by researchers.[17] Instead, notable examples, drawn from between the seventeenth and twentieth centuries, will demonstrate the prevalence of the tontine and its diverse applications. Note that the historical record in some cases is such that it can be difficult to say whether a specific tontine became operational. Nonetheless the prevalence of both operational and proposed tontines indicates that this was an important and widespread financial instrument.

Examples are largely drawn from Europe and the North America. While schemes called 'tontines' still exist in African countries today, these are largely 'chit funds' or rotating loan schemes, and do not employ the tontine principle as defined above.[18] Where appropriate the reader will be directed to more specialised studies. These include works by Moshe Milevsky, David Weir, Robert Jennings and Andrew Trout, and Yikang Li and Casey Rothschild on government tontines in Britain, Ireland and France.[19] David Green's work on the use of tontines to fund civic improvements in Georgian Britain.[20] Diane Clements work on the 1775 Freemasons' Tontine in London, and local studies by James McMahon on the Pery Square Tontine in Limerick and by Sandy Whitnell on the Tontine Hotel in Peebles.[21] And works by Kent McKeever and Phillip Hellwege which draw our attention to the global proliferation of tontines and tontine-type schemes, and their importance during the eighteenth and nineteenth centuries.[22] These are all excellent works should the reader wish to take a deep dive into the topic.

As part life annuity and part life lottery, it is unsurprising that many modern eyes view the tontine with some suspicion. Yet, in the past it was a financial instrument which was applied to diverse projects in various regions across centuries, and one which had a considerable impact on all strata of societies. This may have been directly as a tontine organiser, subscriber, or as the all-important tontine nominee on which ultimate success rested. Or the impact of a tontine may have been less direct, perhaps by patronising a hotel or coffee-room funded by tontine subscriptions, by worshiping in a tontine church, or by traversing a tontine-funded bridge. It may have been that a tontine provided a sickness benefit for a family or paid for a funeral. Even reading a novel or watching a play which referenced the scheme (perhaps in a tontine-funded theatre) would have brought the tontine into the public consciousness. If there is therefore one key takeaway from this book, it is that while it may be a curious thing today, the tontine was far from a historical curio.

Notes

1 *Mercure de France*, Vol. 10, January–June 1726, March (Geneva: Slatkine Reprints, 1968), p.163.

2 D.R. Weir, 'Public Finance, and Revolution in France and England, 1688–1789', *The Journal of Economic History*, Vol. 49, No. 1 (March, 1989), p.113 and p.118; M. Milevsky, *King William's Tontine: Why the Retirement Annuity of the Future Should Resemble Its Past* (Cambridge: Cambridge University Press, 2015), p.98.

3 As we will go into in more detail, tontines often grouped nominees together in age brackets called classes.

4 *Mercure de France*, Vol. 10, January–June 1726, March (Geneva: Slatkine Reprints, 1968), p.163; and P. Sagnac, 'Le crédit de l'État et les banquiers à la fin du XVIIe et au commencement du XVIIIe siècle', *Revue d'histoire moderne et contemporaine* (1899–1914), Vol. 10, No. 4 (1908), p.258; as outlined in 'A Note on Money and Inflation', saying exactly how much this equates to today is difficult.

5 R.L. Stevenson and L. Osbourne, *The Wrong Box* (London: Longmans, Green & Co., 1889); A. Christie, *4.50 from Paddington* (London: Collins Crime Club, 1957); and *The Simpsons*, 'Raging Abe Simpson and His Grumbling Grandson in "The Curse of the Flying Hellfish"', Season 7, Episode 22, 1996; there are also a good number of other works, including; P.G. Wodehouse, *Something Fishy* (London: Herbert Jenkins, 1957); T.B. Constain, *The Tontine*, Vol. 1 (New York: Doubleday and Company, 1955); H.H. Smart, *The Great Tontine* (London: Ward, Lock, and Co., 1881); and any number of tv shows which have used the scheme as a plot device.

6 See, E. Queen, 'The Inner Circle' (1946), in D.S. Davis (ed), *A Choice of Murders*, (New York: Charles Scribner's Sons, 1958), pp. 75-95; and A. Christie, *4.50 from Paddington* (London, 1957); 'The Wild Wild West', 'The Night of the Tottering Tontine', Season 2, Episode 16, 1966.

7 Moshe Milevsky suggests that the more common offence was fraud, where subscribers coerced a child to impersonate another child nominee who had died; see M. Milevsky, *King William's Tontine: Why the Retirement Annuity of the Future Should Resemble Its Past* (Cambridge: Cambridge University Press, 2015), p.86.

8 While modern uses of the tontine principle exist, as this is a history of the scheme it will consider it in the past tense.

9 In Britian the law was tightened up with the Life Assurance Act of 1774 (Chapter 48, 14, Geo 3), part of which legislated to stop policyholders taking out life insurance, and effectively betting on the lives, of people they had legitimate interest in, a tontine nominee could literally be anyone the subscriber chose.

10 In cases where the nominee outlived the subscriber, the tontine share may be inherited by the nominee or another beneficiary.

11 S. Mancuso, 'Tontines and other Forms of Rotating Credit Associations in Africa', in P. Hellwege (ed.), *The Past, Present, and Future of Tontines: A Seventeenth Century Financial Product and the Development of Life Insurance* (Berlin: Duncker & Humblot, 2018), pp.343–366.

12 D.R. Weir, 'Public Finance, and Revolution in France and England, 1688–1789', *The Journal of Economic History*, Vol. 49, No. 1 (March: Cambridge University Press, 1989), p.105; the British tontine of 1757 was cancelled due to poor uptake.

13 M. Milevsky, *King William's Tontine: Why the Retirement Annuity of the Future Should Resemble Its Past* (Cambridge: Cambridge University Press, 2015), p.236;

E. Halley, 'An Estimate of the Degrees of the Mortality of Mankind, Drawn from Curious Tables of the Births and Funerals at the City of Breslaw, with an Attempt to Ascertain the Price of Annuities upon Lives', in *Philosophical Transactions of the Royal Society*, Vol.17, Issue 196, (London, 1693), pp.596–610; and A. Smith, *An Enquiry into the Nature and Causes of the Wealth of Nations*, Book 5, Chapter 3 (London: T. Nelson, 1852), p.390.

14 See, A. McDiarmid, '"Hardly a Kent Name Absent": Raising Capital in Scotland via Tontine, 1775–1850', *Journal of Scottish Historical Studies*, Vol. 43, No. 1 (2023), pp.31–53; and A. McDiarmid, 'The Tontine and the Public Sphere: Ireland and Scotland Compared, 1772–1850', *Genevan Risk and Insurance Review* (2024).

15 The earliest appears to have been to build assembly rooms in Bristol in 1754; C.M. Norris, *The Financing of John Wesley's Methodism C.1740–1800* (Oxford: Oxford University Press, 2017), p.3; shares were priced at £30 each and 120 were sold; and the last was a proposal for an opera house on the Thames embankment in London; D. Green, 'Tontines, Annuities and Civic Improvements in Georgian Britain', *Urban History*, Vol. 46 (2019), p.680 and Appendix 1, pp.681–694 – *Monmouthshire Merlin*, February 12, 1870, p.8; and *Wrexham Guardian*, August 23, 1879, p.3.

16 A. McDiarmid, 'The Development of Mutual Aid Tontines in Nineteenth Century Ireland', *Irish Economic and Social History*, (2024)

17 Research continues to uncover previously unknown schemes, sometimes they are not called tontines but follow the same principle; For example, see K. McKeever, 'Tontines in Portugal – Nicholas Bourey's Paleo-Tontine of 1641', in P. Hellwege (ed.), *The Past, Present, and Future of Tontines: A Seventeenth Century Financial Product and the Development of Life Insurance* (Berlin: Duncker & Humblot, 2018), pp.193–202.

18 K. McKeever, 'A Short History of Tontines', *Fordham Journal of Corporate and Financial Law*, Vol. 15, Issue 42, (2009), pp.516–517.

19 See Y. Li and C. Rothschild, 'Adverse Selection and Redistribution in the Irish Tontines of 1773, 1775, and 1777', *Journal of Risk & Insurance, The American Risk and Insurance Association*, Vol. 87, No. 3 (2020), pp.719–750; R.M. Jennings and A.P. Trout, 'The Irish Tontine (1777) and Fifty Genevans: An Essay on Comparative Morality', *Journal of European Economic History*,Vol. 12, Issue 3, (1983), pp.611–618; and C. Gautier, 'Un investissement Genevois: La tontine d'Irlande de 1977', *Bulletin de la Société d'Histoire et d'Archéologie de Genève,* Vol. 10 (1951), pp.53–57; M. Milevsky, *King William's Tontine: Why the Retirement Annuity of the Future Should Resemble Its Past* (Cambridge: Cambridge University Press, 2015); and D.R. Weir, 'Public Finance, and Revolution in France and England, 1688–1789', *The Journal of Economic History*, Vol. 49, No. 1 (March, 1989), pp.95–124.

20 D. Green, 'Tontines, Annuities and Civic Improvements in Georgian Britain', *Urban History*, Vol. 46 (2019), pp.649–694.

21 D. Clements, 'Invested in Identity: The Freemason's Tontine of 1775' (unpublished thesis), Institute of Historical Research, University of London (2018); J. McMahon, *The Pery Square Tontine* (Limerick: Limerick Civic Trust in association with Fás, 1999); and S. Whitnell, *'The Public Rooms of the County': The History of the Tontine Hotel, Peebles 1803–1890* (Peebles: n.p., 2019).

22 K. McKeever, 'A Short History of Tontines', *Fordham Journal of Corporate and Financial Law* (2009), pp.490–521; P. Hellwege (ed.), *The Past, Present, and Future of Tontines: A Seventeenth Century Product and the Development of Life Insurance* (Berlin: Duncker & Humblot, 2018); and P. Hellwege, *A History of Tontines in Germany: From a Multi-purpose Financial Product to a Single-purpose Pension Product* (Berlin: Duncker & Humblot, 2018).

Bibliography

Primary Sources

Christie, A., *4.50 from Paddington* (London: Collins Crime Club, 1957).

Constain, T.B., *The Tontine*, Vol. 1 (New York: Doubleday and Company, 1955).

Halley, E., 'An Estimate of the Degrees of the Mortality of Mankind, Drawn from Curious Tables of the Births and Funerals at the City of Breslaw, with an Attempt to Ascertain the Price of Annuities upon Lives', in *Philosophical Transactions of the Royal Society*, Vol, 17, Issue 196, (London, 1693), pp. 596–610.

Lesage, A-R, *La Tontine*, translated by F.J. Morlock (Chapel Hill, 2004)

Mercure de France, 'Morts, Naissances, Mariages' Vol. 10, January–June 1726 (Geneva: Slatkine Reprints, 1968).

Smith, A, *The Wealth of Nations*, Vol. 2, Book 5 (London, 1776).

Stevenson, R.L. and Osbourne, L., *The Wrong Box* (LondonLongmans, Green & Co., 1889).

The Simpsons, 'Raging Abe Simpson and His Grumbling Grandson in "The Curse of the Flying Hellfish"', Season 7, Episode 22, 1996.

Queen, E., 'The Inner Circle' (1946), in D.S. Davis (ed), *A Choice of Murders*, (New York: Charles Scribner's Sons, 1958), pp. 75–95

Books

Clements, D., 'Invested in Identity: The Freemason's Tontine of 1775' (unpublished thesis), Institute of Historical Research, University of London (2018).

Hellwege, P., *A History of Tontines in Germany: From a Multi-purpose Financial Product to a Single-purpose Pension Product* (Berlin: Duncker & Humblot, 2018).

McMahon, J., *The Pery Square Tontine* (Limerick: Limerick Civic Trust in association with Fás, 1999).

Milevsky, M., *King William's Tontine: Why the Retirement Annuity of the Future Should Resemble Its Past* (Cambridge: Cambridge University Press, 2015).

Smart, H.H., *The Great Tontine* (London: Ward, Lock, and Co., 1881).

Whitnell, S., *'The Public Rooms of the County': The History of the Tontine Hotel, Peebles 1803–1890* (Peebles: n.p., 2019).

Wodehouse, P.G., *Something Fishy* (London: Herbert Jenkins, 1957).

Edited Collections and Journal Articles

Gautier, C., 'Un investissement Genevois: La tontine d'Irlande de 1977', *Bulletin de la Société d'Histoire et d'Archéologie de Genève*, Vol. 10 (1951), pp.53–57.

Green, D., 'Tontines, annuities and civic improvements in Georgian Britain', *Urban History*, Vol. 46 (2019), pp.649–694.

Hellwege, P. (ed.), *The Past, Present, and Future of Tontines: A Seventeenth Century Product and the Development of Life Insurance* (Berlin: Duncker & Humblot, 2018).

Jennings, R.M. and Trout, A.P., 'The Irish Tontine (1777) and Fifty Genevans: An Essay on Comparative Morality', *Journal of European Economic History*, Vol. 12, Issue 3, (1983), pp.611–618.

Li, Y. and Rothschild, C., 'Adverse Selection and Redistribution in the Irish Tontines of 1773, 1775, and 1777', *Journal of Risk & Insurance, the American Risk and Insurance Association*, Vol. 87, No. 3 (2020), pp.719–750.

Mancuso, S., 'Tontines and other Forms of Rotating Credit Associations in Africa', in Hellwege, P. (ed.), *The Past, Present, and Future of Tontines: A Seventeenth Century Financial Product and the Development of Life Insurance* (Berlin: Duncker & Humblot, 2018), pp.343–366.

McDiarmid, A., '"Hardly a Kent Name Absent": Raising Capital in Scotland via Tontine, 1775–1850', *Journal of Scottish Historical Studies*, Vol. 43, No. 1 (2023), pp.31–53.

McDiarmid, A., 'The Development of Mutual Aid Tontines in Nineteenth Century Ireland', *Irish Economic and Social History* (Online publication at present: https://journals.sagepub.com/doi/10.1177/03324893241243022).

McDiarmid, A., 'The Tontine and the Public Sphere: Ireland and Scotland Compared, 1772–1850', *Genevan Risk and Insurance Review* (2024).

McKeever, K., 'A Short History of Tontines', *Fordham Journal of Corporate and Financial Law*, Vol. 15, Issue 42, (2009), pp.491–521.

McKeever, K., 'Tontines in Portugal – Nicholas Bourey's Paleo-Tontine of 1641', in P. Hellwege (ed.), *The Past, Present, and Future of Tontines: A Seventeenth Century Financial Product and the Development of Life Insurance* (Berlin, 2018), pp.191–202.

Sagnac, P., 'Le crédit de l'État et les banquiers à la fin du XVIIe et au commencement du XVIIIe siècle', in *Revue d'histoire moderne et contemporaine* (1899–1914), Vol. 10, No. 4 (1908), pp.257–272.

Weir, D.R., 'Public Finance, and Revolution in France and England, 1688–1789', *The Journal of Economic History*, Vol. 49, No. 1 (March, 1989), pp.95–124.

'The Wild Wild West', 'The Night of the Tottering Tontine', Season 2, Episode 16, 1966.

2 The Origins and Early Examples of the Tontine

1602–1699

If you had found yourself in the position of subscribing to a seventeenth-century tontine, then you could have done worse than naming Lorenzo de Tonti as your nominee. Born around 1602, in what we would recognise today as south-east Italy, and dying in 1684, Tonti demonstrated a longevity which matched the financial instrument which took his name. The details of his life are relatively obscure. This is partly due to Tonti's own loose relationship with the truth, and partly due to the quality of existing records. References to Tonti in contemporary literature can be uncertain, and other than his tontine proposals and some private correspondence, the sources directly connected to the Italian are sparse. If our subject had been Tonti's eldest son, Henri, an explorer who accompanied Sieur de La Salle into the interior of North America during the 1670s, then we would have Henri's own writings and secondary works from across the nineteenth and twentieth centuries.[1] Henri's brother, Alphonse, meanwhile, was second in command to famed French explorer, Antoine Cadillac and helped to establish the first European settlement at Detroit, Michigan, where he fathered the first European child born there.[2] In written works, Alphonse's name comes up alongside other Italian luminaries in American history, including Christopher Columbus and Amerigo Vespucci.[3] Unfortunately, details of Lorenzo's life have not been so well-preserved for posterity.

While a comprehensive biography is yet to be written about Tonti Sr., recent work by Christian Rietsch and George Gallais-Hamonno, as well as that undertaken by Robert Jennings and Andrew Trout in the early 1980s, has shone a light on some of the more colourful aspects of his life.[4] And while there remains some disagreement over basic details, such as Tonti's exact date of birth, his birth name, and some confusion over how many sons he had, from what we do know, it is clear that Tonti was of a practical, if often deceitful, disposition.[5]

From a young age, Tonti, who was likely baptised Lorenzo Baroncini, later changing his name and claiming to be a relative of the esteemed Michealangelo Cardinal Tonti (1566–1622), dealt in information.[6] He worked as an embroiderer in the household of Paolo Giordano II Orsini, Duke of Bracciano, where he used his access to spy on the family. In the mid-1630s Tonti then

DOI: 10.4324/9781003491002-2

entered the service of Manuel de Acevedo y Zúñiga, the Count of Monterey, and Spanish viceroy between 1631 and 1637. His allegiance was fleeting, however, and as the viceroy's tenure in office was coming to an end, Tonti was enlisted by the incoming official to spy on Monterey.[7] This pattern continued, with Tonti spending the last years of the 1630s gathering information for Duke Ludovisio, the nephew of Pope Urban VIII (1623–1644). For this Tonti earned 100 crowns a year, and through the duke's good graces was appointed to govern the southern Italian town of Rossano in the early 1640s. His time in office was short-lived, as the local population soon came to detest Tonti for his 'alleged acts of theft'.[8] Following this he exploited some confusion around the existence of at least two Italian noble families with the surname of Tonti, and appropriated noble titles to which he had no right.[9]

In 1647, at the time of a successful revolt against Spanish power in Naples, Tonti passed information to Pope Innocent X (1644–1655) and to the French ambassador in Rome, who fed back to chief minister Cardinal Mazarin and the French court in Paris.[10] In Naples he became an important adviser to the Duke of Guise, the leader of the republic formed after the revolution, for which he was granted several pensions, and became Mazarin's agent in the region. Praise for Tonti, often equivocal, was forthcoming from those who mattered. Guise described him as 'of low birth, but with some cunning', while Henri Abbot Arnauld, the French representative in Rome, commended Tonti's intellect.[11] Tonti must have felt untouchable, because despite his pensions, he supplemented his income with a series of thefts, frauds, and illicit practices. Trust in Tonti quickly diminished, he came to be viewed in Naples as rapacious and scheming, even Mazarin determined him to be 'capable of any evilness'.[12] Despite this judgement, when the short-lived Neapolitan Republic collapsed and Tonti was forced to flee the region, it was France and Mazarin that provided him with refuge.

In France, Tonti furnished the cardinal with economic advice and financial schemes intended to raise state revenue but was by no means a financial genius. As Jennings and Trout have concluded from their work on Tonti's papers and his writings, he was a 'stranger to economic reality, a man with unmitigated gall and an oversimplified approach to finance, busily marketing panaceas to worried statesmen'.[13] Yet here we are almost 400 years on from his first tontine proposal still talking about Tonti.

The truth, however, is that until someone writes a biography, the scholarly focus is not really on Tonti, but rather the tontine. What we know about his life has largely been told in fragments, to provide context in the works of scholars more interested in the eponymous financial scheme which overshadows the man himself. The tontine is, after all, Lorenzo de Tonti's legacy. Or is it?

Unfortunately for Tonti, in recent years scholars have been at pains to inform us that he was not the originator of the principle which underpins the tontine concept. Moshe Milevsky's excellent work on the first English government tontine of 1693 sought to dispel several myths around the scheme. The first of which was that 'tontines were probably not invented by Tonti'.[14] Milevsky drew attention to an English will written in 1581, at least 20 years before Tonti was born, in which the testator's beneficiaries were provided for via a tontine-type scheme. The beneficiaries were comprised of eleven servants – one of whom was likely William Shakespeare! – who each received a yearly pension which increased as the other beneficiaries died.[15] Jennings and Trout have meanwhile determined that Tonti's idea was 'a refinement of *rentes viageres*, or lifetime annuities', which had existed in France since at least the sixteenth century.[16] While others suggest Tonti borrowed the idea from the *Monte delle doti*, a medieval Italian investment fund which allowed parents to save a dowry for their daughter.[17] This included a tontine-like function which in the event of a daughter dying or marrying before the age of 18, would allow the accumulated sum to be paid to a younger daughter, and if there was no younger daughter then it would revert to the scheme organisers and be shared among other participants.[18]

Two of the most devastating blows to Tonti's legacy in recent years have come from the works of Maura Fortunati and Kent McKeever. Fortunati uncovered a 'tontine' plan presented to the Duke of Savoy in the 1630s or 1640s, at least a decade before Tonti's first plan.[19] While Mckeever, highlighted a Portuguese proposal put to the Lisbon senate in 1641 by Nicolas Bourey, a French or Belgian merchant, for a revenue raising scheme with a basic tontine principle.[20] Each of these projects was a tontine in all but name.

So, what does this mean for the history of the tontine? Well, it means that before Tonti 'invented' the tontine, that other financial instruments with a similar purpose existed. But does it really matter who invented it? As Stephen Stigler's playfully named 'Stigler's Law of Eponymy' states 'no scientific discovery is named after its original discoverer'.[21] What is important is that after Tonti wrote his proposal in the early 1650s, the tontine became increasingly popular across Europe and North America in the centuries which followed. And the framework which Tonti suggested, with some developments, became the standard for future tontines. For these reasons, Tonti is, and will always be, as Robert Louis Stevenson and Lloyd Osbourne affirmed in the 1889 novel, *The Wrong Box*, 'the ass that started tontines'.[22]

Tonti's Tontine

By the late 1640s, Tonti was in the orbit of Mazarin. Elevated to cardinal in 1642, Mazarine, also an Italian and of a similar age to Tonti, was for a short period chief minister to Louis XIII (r.1610–1643). Following Louis' death at the age of 41 in 1643 (the French king would not have been a profitable tontine nominee), Mazarin continued as chief minister, heading the government of his widow, Anne of Austria. Anne was regent for the new king, a young

Louis XIV (r.1643–1715), but it was Mazarin who had the power.[23] The cardinal granted Tonti a 6,000 livres annual pension, for which he provided largely financial advice in return.[24] Tonti proposed state lotteries and recommended ways to aid domestic silk production. He prepared guidance on how to make the French East India Company the most powerful in Europe within a year.[25] And there was of course the tontine, which Tonti first presented to Mazarin in 1652.[26]

At this time France was in dire need of money. The country's participation in the Thirty Years' War (1618–1648) had levied a heavy cost to both French lives and to the country's finances.[27] In 1648 the Peace of Westphalia brought the war to an end, but hostilities continued for France, with the Franco-Spanish War (1635–1659) persisting for a further 11 years.[28] As a result, the national debt had risen steadily during the first half of the seventeenth century, hitting 600 million livres by the time Mazarine came to office in 1642.[29] Continuing the legacy of his predecessor, Armand du Plessis (Cardinal Richelieu, chief minister between 1624 and 1642), Mazarine employed 'coercive government to impose unprecedented fiscal burdens' on the French people, forcibly reducing the national debt to around half, setting the interest which the government would pay at four per cent, and levying heavy taxes.[30] By 1648, opposition to Mazarine's policies erupted into revolt, as a series of civil wars broke out in the country.[31] Fighting took place in fits and starts over the next five years, in which the government was pitted against an opposition comprised of nobility, lawmakers, and regular French citizens.

While Mazarin and the French crown emerged victorious in 1653, the financial problems facing the country continued to escalate. The tax collection system of the seventeenth-century French crown was ineffective, and any money that came in quickly went out to cover the cost of war or to service outstanding debt.[32] To raise extra money the crown imposed special taxes on particularly wealthy French citizens; it sold public offices for revenue; and it exacted fines against lawbreakers where they could. The crown also sold annuities, frequently under-pricing these, and it borrowed funds from private lenders, often under unfavourable terms.[33] So, when Tonti pitched his modified life annuity as being capable of raising 20 million livres in 1652, this was a significant sum for of money for the struggling French administration.

It is important that we should acknowledge that the original tontine was not a great investment. It certainly could be if your nominee outlived the others in their class, as the case of Madame Barbier in the preceding chapter demonstrated, but it was never promoted as a pension for subscribers (this would come much later). Instead, Tonti's intention, as Milevsky has stated, was:

> to make it easier and cheaper for the king or queen or Parliament (or any other government entity) to borrow money[34]

And as part lottery, part life annuity, the tontine was designed to appeal to subscribers by giving them the opportunity, not necessarily the reality, of high returns. In Tonti's model the crown got immediate access to the fund raised via tontine, and in return it guaranteed a fixed yearly repayment amount which was divided and paid to active subscribers, and which increased as nominees died. The crown's financial commitment then ended when all nominees were dead.

Without getting too into the financial weeds, here is what Tonti proposed. 20 million livres would be raised through the sale of 66,000 shares priced at 300 livres each. Each subscriber would start with an annuity of five per cent (15 livres per share), which would be secured against a nominated life. The nominees were often young family members of the subscriber, or in some cases public figures were selected. George III was for instance a popular choice in the British tontine of 1789; the king died at the age of 81 in 1820 and provided a reasonable return. In contrast, a 21-year-old Marie Antoinette was nominated in the 1777 Irish government tontine by a subscriber who was not to know that the young French queen would lose her head at the guillotine in 1793.[35]

To provide some fairness to subscribers, Tonti separated the nominees into ten age classes. These went from class 1, children aged 0–7 years of age, and increased in 7-year increments to class 10, adults aged 63 and over.[36] Each subscriber would only benefit if a nominee died in the class in which they also had a nominee, and each class was self-contained, finishing when all nominees from that age group had died. Tonti's tontine was therefore ten individual tontines running concurrently. It is worth noting, however, that regardless of the class, every subscriber commenced the scheme with an annuity of five per cent. This meant that at the basic rate, it would take a subscriber 20 years to recover their initial investment ($5 \times 20 = 100$). This could of course be quicker depending on the mortality rate, but offering class 10 (63 and above), a group statistically more likely to die, the same rate as class 1 (0–7), was not a good deal for investors. The simplicity of Tonti's proposal was something that would become a problem.

The tontine required a commitment from the French administration to pay a total 1 million livres in repayments, plus 25,000 livres in overheads, per annum for the 10 classes. Tonti stood to make a considerable sum from the scheme. Of the 25,000 livres ringfenced to cover the administration of the project, half of this was to recompense any expenses incurred by the French finance minister and his employees, from which Tonti would presumably get his share. In addition, the French crown issued a patent which granted Tonti one tenth of all the sums subscribed in all classes of the tontine, potentially netting him 2 million livres.[37]

Tonti wasn't just about the money, however. His proposal also professed concern for the wellbeing of the family unit and wider society, and made the case that this could be improved through the tontine. He claimed that by purchasing just a few shares in the tontine, parents could guarantee the future wealth of their children. This was highlighted as being particularly significant for daughters, who could become independently wealthy and thus secure an advantageous marriage. In addition, he argued that regular income from the tontine could improve the mental health of young people, who, for want of money, were often forced into professions that did not suit them and which threw them into 'despair'. When it came to family relationships, Tonti reasoned that the tontine would motivate husbands and wives to 'take extremely good care of each other', and that parents and children would love and care for one another more, driven by the 'advantages everyone will find in living a long life'. The tontine, Tonti claimed, would bring the generations closer together, and that rather than the old being 'resented by those eagerly awaiting [their] death', they would, if named as nominees be looked after and treated with 'respect and care because of the advantage they will find and will hope to increase'.[38] Ok, so perhaps Tonti was all about the money!

It may be at this point that readers expect to be told that Tonti's proposal was quickly accepted by the French administration and went on to be a runaway success. It was certainly supported by the French crown, with a series of royal orders printed during 1652 and 1653 endorsing the project.[39] Mazarin also enthused that the scheme was 'une mine d'or pour le Roi' (a gold mine for the king). Yet, despite the great riches promised by Tonti, the tontine failed to be registered by the *Parlement de Paris*, and was not developed any further at this time.[40] The rejection was driven by three main reasons. (1) The actual cost of the tontine to the state was impossible to calculate; (2) The belief that whatever the costs may be, they would be very high; and (3) The starting interest rate of five per cent for all nominees was too low, certainly when compared to that which was being offered on life annuities.[41] A sceptical public response to the venture also appears to have been an issue.

In the years which followed the *Parlement's* rejection, Tonti continued to revise his scheme. In 1656, a second unsuccessful attempt at establishing a French tontine emerged, this time under the name of the 'Royal Bank', which was similarly left wanting when it came to public support.[42] Then in 1660, Tonti proposed an ecclesiastical tontine, designed to clear the debts of the French clergy. He promoted the scheme and himself fiercely at this time, using the noble titles he had misappropriated in the mid-1640s, and positioned himself as comptroller general of the new tontine.[43] In 1663 he wrote to Jean-Baptiste Colbert, who after Mazarin's death in 1661 had risen to chief minister of France, proposing a tontine be established in Brittany, and four years later in 1667 he proposed a tontine for the province of Languedoc.[44] All of Tonti's proposals failed.

The death of Mazarin in March 1661 was a blow for Tonti. His generous 6,000 livres pension all but stopped. He petitioned the king in early 1663 on the matter, and in October of that year he complained to Colbert that he had received a total of only 3,000 livres between 1660 and 1663. At this time Tonti was supporting a family of 17 and was being hounded by his creditors, whom he feared would have him imprisoned. He had hoped that his tontine would have made him rich, but with each rejection the likelihood of this slipped away. To improve his condition, Tonti drew on his earlier experience as a spy and wrote to the Spanish ambassador with an offer. He proposed to provoke unrest in France and provide the ambassador with inside knowledge on Louis XIV and anything else he could on foreign monarchs.[45] Unfortunately for Tonti, the letter was intercepted by the French government. As a result, he was arrested and imprisoned in the Bastille in January 1668.

Following his incarceration, things went from bad to worse for Tonti. Two of his sons were also embroiled in his attempted intrigue and followed him to the Bastille a month later.[46] Then in March 1669, he was given the news that his wife had died. Tonti's financial woes also continued, and even worsened, with the requirement that he pay for his stay in gaol, borrowing money with which to buy his own food and clothes.[47] Tonti spent seven years in the Bastille before being released. He died in 1684, having never managed to monetise his tontine scheme.

European Tontines, 1653–1689

In the years between Tonti's proposal and the first French government tontine of 1689, several successful and unsuccessful tontines emerged from mainland Europe. The earliest was in Denmark, and occurred at the same time as Tonti was trying to establish his own scheme in France. The man behind the plan was Poul Klingenberg, a native of Hamburg who became Postmaster General of Denmark in 1654. There have been claims that Klingenberg met Tonti in 1652 and was so impressed by the model that he convinced Frederik III of Denmark (r.1648–1670) to implement a tontine.[48] There is, however, no primary source evidence to confirm this meeting, and it is more likely they had indirect contact via an acquaintance.[49] Klingenberg's scheme sought to raise 1,600,000 rigsdaler through the sale of 16,000 shares and was certainly inspired by Tonti's. It separated nominees into separate classes and paid all subscribers a starting interest rate of five per cent.[50] Unfortunately for Klingenberg the proposal was like Tonti's in another way, in that it failed to ignite any significant public interest and was abandoned.[51] A second attempt at establishing a Danish tontine was attempted in 1694 and was likewise abandoned.[52]

In German and German-speaking territories, Phillip Hellwege has identified 18 'tontines or tontine plans', largely operated by public bodies, between the 1650s and 1750. These were supplemented with tontines issued by pension fund organisers between the 1770s and 1830s and further tontine life insurance products in the nineteenth century.[53] Of the schemes identified by Hellwege, only four were prior to 1700, and not all were successful.

Here the earliest attempts to establish tontines were in the city of Gdańsk.[54] The first was in 1657, as the municipality sought to raise 100,000 florins, through the sale of 1,000 shares offering six per cent interest, which was to be directed into the city's budget. At 100 florins a share, the price was too high for many investors, leading to a revision which cut the subscription price in half. Even after this there is no evidence that the scheme went ahead. 31 years later the government of the city tried again. The plan in 1688, which hoped to raise 347,625 florins, was more complicated than the first and staggered the price of the shares depending on the age of the nominee. For example, those with the youngest nominees (0–20 years of age) would pay 1,000 florins per share, while those with the oldest (80 and above) would pay 300 florins each. Even with this innovation, the tontine plan was unsuccessful.[55]

There are also cases of schemes operating in German territories which used the tontine principle, but not which were not called tontines. An interesting example of this was a 1692 loan agreement in the northwestern city of Bremen. This was a relatively straight forward loan, in which a consortium of 10 lenders agreed to lend the city 1,000 thalers at four per cent interest. The tontine aspect was a feature distinct from the loan and was part of a private agreement between the lenders. This required each lender to name a nominee against whose life repayments were secured. Each year the lender or their heirs would then only receive their share if the nominee was alive; this would then increase as the number of nominees reduced. While the word 'tontine' was never used by the group, the linking of loan repayments to benefit of survivorship was an example of the tontine principle.[56] Then in Prussia six years later, the first operational scheme that might justifiably be called a public tontine in the German territories was offered. This consisted of only one class of nominee (all under 18 years of age) and raised 100,000 thalers via 1,000 shares to be directed at the state's military budget.[57] While the scheme offered subscribers an initial interest rate of five per cent with benefit of survivorship, it was not marketed as a tontine, but as a life annuity.[58]

Moving slightly west, the tontine was used extensively in the Dutch Republic. There the scheme existed as a tool of local government, semi-public bodies, and as a popular private instrument.[59] The first was issued by the municipality of Kampen in 1670 and raised 100,000 guilders across 400 shares. It proved to be a success and inspired several other schemes across the region; these included tontines in Amsterdam and Groningen (1670), Middleburg (1671), and Delft (1673).[60] The tontine quickly developed into a popular tool of Dutch local government, with as many as 60 tontines issued by public corporations between 1670 and 1869. The estates of Holland also considered issuing tontines in 1670 and 1735, but on both occasions decided against it.[61]

The success of tontines offered by public bodies in the Dutch Republic was mirrored, and indeed exceeded, by the private tontine schemes which became incredibly popular in the region around the end of the seventeenth century. These brought together a group of subscribers, usually numbering between 10 and 30, although some had as many as 50 participants, and invested the principal sum raised via tontine into some form of securities. A popular choice was to invest in stock of the Dutch East India Company, but later expanded to include a variety of bonds issued by central and provincial governments, with some tontine schemes diversifying their securities portfolio.[62] Like other tontines, a subscriber's participation required their nominee's life to be ongoing, and if this was the case, the interest or dividends paid on the securities was divided among active subscribers. The first of these private tontines was established in 1670, and by 1700 almost 200 had been set up.[63] The appetite for such ventures was slowed slightly when a fraud scandal involving the manager of a large number of tontine schemes erupted in 1703. But even with this, at least 100 tontines of this sort went on to be set up in the Dutch Republic during the next century.[64]

This form of private investment tontine was also reasonably popular in England during the last quarter of the eighteenth century but appears to have been relatively rare prior to this. Certainly, in the late seventeenth century only two examples can be found, both linked to the City of London. The first appeared in 1674 and worked to Tonti's model but was likely also influenced by the Dutch examples.[65] It proposed that nominees be divided into ten classes which were nearly identical to Tonti's.[66] Shares were priced at £20 each, and subscribers were allowed to have as many shares taken out on the one life as they pleased.[67] The second proposal appeared nine years later in 1683. This scheme sought to raise £100,000 across ten classes, offering all subscribers an initial six per cent interest. The pricing structure was a little unusual and worked on a sliding scale. Each of the ten classes would contribute 10,000 to the total, but through a different number of subscriber shares. Class 1 (0 to under 7) for example, offered 2,000 shares at £5 to make up £10,000, while class 2 (7 to under 14) offered 1,000 shares at £10. The ratio of total shares to share price continued to be adjusted until class 10 (63–70), which priced shares at £1,000 each and limited these to 10 in total. It does not appear that either scheme got off the ground.[68]

The First French and English Government Tontines of 1689–1696

During the 1660s, Colbert managed to put France on a stronger financial footing than had been the case during the previous decade. Aided by the end of the Franco-Spanish War in 1659, he had restored financial solvency to the country.[69] Much of the good work was undone, however, when Louis XIV commenced a conflict with the Dutch Republic in 1672. The French king was keen to command the Spanish-Netherlands (largely modern day Belgium and Luxembourg) an objective which was opposed by the Dutch stadtholder, William of Orange (r.1672–1702). The Franco-Dutch War (1672–1678) lasted for six years, during which time Colbert raised money through the sale of government offices and annuities, with neither side benefiting greatly.[70] A strained peace then existed for the next decade before hostilities again erupted between the two adversaries in the Nine Years' War (1688–1697). It was at this time that Tonti's financial proposal was dusted off and reevaluated.

The first French tontine of 1689 avoided the word 'tontine' in its planning. Presumably Tonti, who had died only five years earlier, was still a disgraced figure. Instead, it was called 'a life annuity with additional benefits of survivorship', but in all its features it was a tontine. The scheme maintained the basic model of Tonti's original plan; investors bought shares priced at 300 livres each secured on nominated lives, the principle was lost but earned annual interest, those with an active nominee shared the aggregate interest for their class, and when the last nominee of a class died the interest reverted to the French state.[71]

The most significant changes implemented for the 1689 tontine from Tonti's original proposal were a narrowing of the age brackets for nominees (expanding these to fourteen classes in five-year increments, as opposed to Tonti's ten classes separated by seven years), and an increase in the interest rates offered to subscribers. The reader will remember that one of the stumbling blocks to Tonti getting the go ahead in 1653 was a concern over the low rate of return for investors. This was now addressed by offering varying rates of return depending on the class of nominee. Classes 1 and 2 (ages 0–5 and 5–10) commenced on five per cent interest, while classes 3 and 4 (10–15 and 15–20) started at a rate of 5.56 per cent. This correlation between the age band of the nominee and an increase in interest rate continued through the classes of the tontine. Classes 9 and 10 (40–45 and 45–50) for example, started on an interest rate of 8.33 per cent, while the oldest class, those aged 65 and above, were given an initial interest rate of 12.5 per cent.[72] On average, this spread meant that the French tontine was paying around nine per cent interest per nominee.[73] The scheme therefore offered an incentive for subscribers to select older nominees. Of course, there was a likelihood they would live for a shorter time than the younger nominees, but the offer of a higher interest rate within a class where mortality would be higher, provided the opportunity for increased returns, albeit for a shorter period.

A second French government scheme followed in 1696, this time it was explicitly called a 'tontine'.[74] The organisation of the scheme expanded to 15 separate classes and introduced 60 subdivisions within these classes.[75] A subdivision being where a class was further divided into a smaller group; in this case each of the main 15 classes was divided into four further groups. This meant that the death of a nominee would only impact the annuity rate of subscribers in the same class and subdivision. Think of it as a tontine, within a tontine, within a tontine. The interest offered was more generous than it had been in 1689, starting at around seven per cent for the youngest nominees up to 14 per cent for the eldest.[76]

While the French government went on to raise more than 118 million livres between 1689 and 1759 via tontine, the two schemes of the late seventeenth century performed poorly.[77] Despite a good deal of optimism around the 1689 tontine, it raised just over 3.6 million livres; little more than 18 per cent of its 19.6 million livres target. The 1696 tontine did a little better by raising just over 20 per cent of its target; although this must be caveated by saying it aimed to raise the lower sum of just over 14 million livres.[78] French public tontines were therefore a slow starter, but as we will see in the next chapter, they certainly picked up the pace during the eighteenth century.

The first English tontine, meanwhile, commenced in 1693. The timing is important, because while the French had a direct connection to the tontine via Tonti, the English did not. It appeared in England against a backdrop of financial development, as the king, William III & II (r.1689–1702), sought to finance his part in the Nine Years' War against France. William wasn't long in the job, having ascended to the throne with his wife, Mary Stewart, after ousting her father, and his uncle, James VII & II (r.1685–1688) in 1688. Termed the 'Glorious Revolution', due to its perceived bloodless nature (although this designation is largely Anglocentric and does not stand up if we consider the revolution in Ireland and Scotland), the event ushered in a form of proto-constitutional monarchy.[79] It also initiated a period of financial innovation, which included a state lottery and the establishment of the Bank of England in 1694, a short-lived land bank in 1696, and the tontine.[80]

The tontine is significant in the history of English state finance for being the point at which the country's National Debt was first established, yet its origins remain unclear. There is a school of thought which argues that as William III was Dutch (William and the aforementioned, Dutch stadtholder, William of Orange, were one and the same), the concept entered England when he did.[81] As already discussed, the tontine had been a popular tool in the Dutch Republic since the 1670s, and no doubt William's financial advisers were well-versed in the scheme.[82] However, as we have also briefly touched on, Milevsky has identified the practice of some English wills including a tontine-structure from at least the 1580s.[83] And as detailed earlier in this chapter, there had been attempts to establish tontines in the City of London in 1674 and 1683. The concept was therefore known in England prior to William's arrival. There is another suggestion, from P.G.M. Dickson, that the 1693 English tontine was the brainchild of Scottish projector, William Paterson.[84] Paterson was certainly in the thick of it at this time, he was a key player in establishing the Bank of England, and was also responsible for the Company of Scotland's attempt to establish a Scottish colony on the Isthmus of Darien in South America. Yet, regardless of who was behind the first English tontine, one thing is for certain, like the earliest French government tontines, it was not a financial success.

The legislation which brought the tontine into being was drafted in 1692 and passed early the next year. Loftily titled the 'Million Act', as it aimed to raise £1 million, Jennings and Trout have described it as 'an abject lesson in how not to design a financial instrument'.[85] It offered subscribers an initial interest rate of 10 per cent, which after seven years reduced to seven per cent (this base rate is separate from any increase that would be applied through the tontine function).[86] These rates were offered regardless of the age of nominee and all nominees were grouped together in a single class. The tontine also planned to freeze the rate of annuity when the scheme was down to its last seven nominees. This meant that subscribers would still receive their annuity, but it would not increase after this.

When shares in the tontine became available for purchase, public response was muted. This was not helped by the English government indicating that if subscriptions fell short, it would offer a 14 per cent life annuity in place of the tontine. This alternative deal, as Edmund Halley stated at the time, and as Milevsky has since shown in detail, was by far the better offer. So while a respectable enough 3,776 shares went on to be bought in the tontine, the majority of these (2695) were quickly transferred into the higher paying life annuity.[87] This left 1,081 shares in the tontine, leaving a total fund of £108, 100, just over 10 per cent of the intended target.[88]

While early French and English tontines had similar difficulties in successfully establishing themselves, it must be made clear that these were very different offerings. First, all French and English (and later Irish) government tontine subscriptions were expensive. The English tontine of 1693 was, however, priced considerably higher than the French schemes of this time. French shares for the 1689 tontine cost 300 livres each, a figure way beyond the means of the average French citizen, but which was far cheaper than English shares priced at £100; if we use Paritius' figures this was equivalent to around 1,334 livres at the beginning of the eighteenth century (see 'A Note on Money and Inflation'). Structurally the English tontine was also a very different proposition. French tontines since Tonti's original proposal had been organised into classes separated by age; the first English tontine eschewed this practice and had only one nominee group. This meant that whether your nominee was 8 or 80, you commenced on the same interest rate and took your chances with everyone else.

That there was no incentive to name older nominees in the English tontine is borne out by more than 93 per cent of this group being under 25 years of age. This is compared to the two French schemes, with under-25s in the 1689 tontine making up 22.4 per cent of nominees, and those in 1696 representing 20.9 per cent of the total.[89] The French, through defined classes and higher rates of interest for older nominees, therefore had a fairer playing field, actuarially speaking. But there are examples in the English tontine which demonstrate the important part played by fortune. There was, for instance a 34-year-old nominee in 1693, Londoner, Jonathon Smith, who lived for another 31 years, and a 36-year-old, Dutch nominee, James Senserfe, who lived until the age of 73. Compare this to eight-year-old, Andrew Slee of Norfolk, who died at age nine, or another Dutch nominee, two-year-old Esther Ximenes, who passed away before her third birthday.[90] So while it might be expected that a young nominee would offer a better return than an older one, and there are of course many examples of young nominees living long lives and providing subscribers with good returns, this was not guaranteed. There were also many occurrences of older nominees proving to be equally profitable, demonstrating just how much of a lottery the tontine could be.

Conclusion

Alas, poor Tonti! During his lifetime, and despite his best efforts, he failed to monetise the financial instrument which took his name. The last decades of his life saw him hunted, and indeed haunted, by his creditors and locked in the Bastille. By the time his 1653 proposal was dusted off to provide the framework for the first French government tontine in 1689 he had been dead for five years. To add insult to injury there was no acknowledgement of Tonti's contribution to the scheme and they did not even call it a tontine.

That said, Tonti does not appear to have been a 'good' man, and from this vantage point it is hard to call him a success. Yet here we are four centuries later still talking about him; few of us will be so fortunate. Undoubtedly, he was optimistic in his projections. His plan to raise 20 million livres in 1653 would have required more than 66,000 shares to be sold; a figure Milevsky doubts was reached in the culminative total for shares sold in all French tontines operated over the next century.[91] Yet his proposal brought him the backing of Mazarin and the French crown, and while it failed to make it beyond the *Parlement de Paris*, this was not the end of the tale. In Tonti's lifetime other regions developed tontines, what he thought about this, if he even knew, is unknown. Then, in the wake of his death in 1684, the tontine emerged as a popular revenue-raising tool with governments, which, as we shall see, was just the start.

Notes

1 H. Tonti, *Dernieres Decouvertes dans L'Amerique Septentrionale de M. De La Sale* (Paris: Jean Guignard, 1697); M.H. Catherwood, *The Story of Tonty* (Chicago: A. C. McClurg and Company, 1890); H.E. Legler, *The Man with the Iron Hand Chevalier Henry de Tonty's Exploits in the Valley of the Mississippi* (Milwaukee: n.p., 1896); E.R. Murphy, *Henry de Tonty, Fur Trader of the Mississippi* (Baltimore: Johns Hopkins Press, 1941); and Jay Higginbotham, 'Henri de Tonti's Mission to the Chickasaw, 1702', *Louisiana History*, Vol. 19 (Summer 1978), pp.285–296.
2 A. Delicato, *Italians in Detroit* (Chicago Arcadia Publishing, 2005), p.30.
3 A. Delicato, *Italians in Detroit* (Chicago Arcadia Publishing, 2005).
4 C. Rietsch and G. Gallais-Hamonno, 'Lorenzo Tonti', in P. Hellwege (ed.), *The Past, Present, and Future of Tontines: A Seventeenth Century Financial Product and the Development of Life Insurance* (Berlin: Duncker & Humblot, 2018), pp.19–47; and R.M. Jennings and A.P Trout, *The Tontine: From the Reign of Louis XIV to the French Revolutionary Era* (Philadelphia: University of Pennsylvania, 1982), pp.4–11.

5 Rietsch and Gallais-Hamonno state Tonti was born in 1602, but acknowledge that some sources state 1603, and others 1620 and 1630, although these later dates are not likely. They also state that Tonti was born Lorenzo Baroncini, although another account claims it was Lorenzo Tontoli. Rietsch and Gallais-Hamonno also claim that Tonti had three children, Henri. Alphonse, and Enrico, and that little is known of the latter. I suggest there is confusion here, and that Enrico is actually Henri; see C. Rietsch and G. Gallais-Hamonno, 'Lorenzo Tonti', in P. Hellwege (ed.), *The Past, Present, and Future of Tontines: A Seventeenth Century Financial Product and the Development of Life Insurance* (Berlin: Duncker & Humblot, 2018), pp.19–25.

6 C. Rietsch and G. Gallais-Hamonno, 'Lorenzo Tonti', in P. Hellwege (ed.), *The Past, Present, and Future of Tontines: A Seventeenth Century Financial Product and the Development of Life Insurance* (Berlin: Duncker & Humblot, 2018), p.21.

7 C. Rietsch and G. Gallais-Hamonno, 'Lorenzo Tonti', in P. Hellwege (ed.), *The Past, Present, and Future of Tontines: A Seventeenth Century Financial Product and the Development of Life Insurance* (Berlin: Duncker & Humblot, 2018), p.21.

8 C. Rietsch and G. Gallais-Hamonno, 'Lorenzo Tonti', in P. Hellwege (ed.), *The Past, Present, and Future of Tontines: A Seventeenth Century Financial Product and the Development of Life Insurance* (Berlin: Duncker & Humblot, 2018), pp.21–22.

9 From 1647 he assumed the titles of 'Roman Gentleman' and 'Knight of Paludi', even passing these on to his sons; C. Rietsch and G. Gallais-Hamonno, 'Lorenzo Tonti', in P. Hellwege (ed.), *The Past, Present, and Future of Tontines: A Seventeenth Century Financial Product and the Development of Life Insurance* (Berlin: Duncker & Humblot, 2018), p.22.

10 C. Rietsch and G. Gallais-Hamonno, 'Lorenzo Tonti', in P. Hellwege (ed.), *The Past, Present, and Future of Tontines: A Seventeenth Century Financial Product and the Development of Life Insurance* (Berlin: Duncker & Humblot, 2018), p.23.

11 C. Rietsch and G. Gallais-Hamonno, 'Lorenzo Tonti', in P. Hellwege (ed.), *The Past, Present, and Future of Tontines: A Seventeenth Century Financial Product and the Development of Life Insurance* (Berlin: Duncker & Humblot, 2018), p.23.

12 C. Rietsch and G. Gallais-Hamonno, 'Lorenzo Tonti', in P. Hellwege (ed.), *The Past, Present, and Future of Tontines: A Seventeenth Century Financial Product and the Development of Life Insurance* (Berlin: Duncker & Humblot, 2018), p.24.

13 R.M. Jennings and A.P Trout, *The Tontine: From the Reign of Louis XIV to the French Revolutionary Era* (Philadelphia: University of Pennsylvania, 1982), p.7.

14 M. Milevsky, *King William's Tontine: Why the Retirement Annuity of the Future Should Resemble Its Past* (Cambridge: Cambridge University Press, 2015), p.40.

15 M. Milevsky, *King William's Tontine: Why the Retirement Annuity of the Future Should Resemble Its Past* (Cambridge: Cambridge University Press, 2015), pp.37–40.

16 R.M. Jennings and A.P. Trout, 'The Tontine Re-examined: A Modest Proposal to Reduce the National Debt', *Economy and History*, Vol. 17, No. 1 (1974), p.106; and Alexander Hamilton's Tontine Proposal Author(s): Robert M. Jennings, Donald F. Swanson and Andrew P. Trout Source: *The William and Mary Quarterly*, Vol. 45, No. 1 (January, 1988), pp.107–115.

17 C. Rietsch and G. Gallais-Hamonno, 'Lorenzo Tonti', in P. Hellwege (ed.), *The Past, Present, and Future of Tontines: A Seventeenth Century Financial Product and the Development of Life Insurance* (Berlin: Duncker & Humblot, 2018), p.27.

18 J. Atack and L. Neal, *The Origins and Development of Financial Markets and Institutions: From the Seventeenth Century to the Present* (Cambridge: Cambridge University Press, 2009), p.90; M. Milevsky, *King William's Tontine: Why the Retirement Annuity of the Future Should Resemble Its Past* (Cambridge: Cambridge University Press, 2015), p.46; Jennings and Trout do, however, come to Tonti's defence here, and state that there is a 'long step' between these funds to provide a daughter with a

dowry, and the large-scale national financial instrument Tonti would propose in 1652, see, R.M. Jennings and A.P. Trout, *The Tontine: From the Reign of Louis XIV to the French Revolutionary Era* (Philadelphia: University of Pennsylvania, 1982), p.4.

19 M. Fortunati, 'Tontines in Italy', in P. Hellwege (ed.), *The Past, Present, and Future of Tontines: A Seventeenth Century Financial Product and the Development of Life Insurance* (Berlin: Duncker & Humblot, 2018), p.213.

20 K. McKeever, 'Tontines in Portugal – Nicholas Bourey's Paleo-Tontine of 1641', in P. Hellwege, *The Past, Present, and Future of Tontines: A Seventeenth Century Financial Product and the Development of Life Insurance* (Berlin: Duncker & Humblot, 2018), pp.191–201; The scheme offered an initial five per cent interest on all shares, increasing as nominees died. It did not, however, separate nominees into separate age groups as Tonti would later do. Whether there was any connection between Bouray and Tonti is unknown. It may be, as McKeever states, a case of 'simultaneous invention' in which two unconnected individuals created the same scheme. p.201

21 Stigler actually credits sociologist Robert K. Merton with the formulation; S. Stigler, *Statistics on the Table: The History of Statistical Concepts and Methods* (Boston: Harvard University Press, 2002), pp.277–290.

22 R.L. Stevenson and L. Osbourne, *The Wrong Box* (LondonLongmans, Green & Co., 1889), p.65.

23 G. Treasure, *Mazarin: The Crisis of Absolutism in France* (London: Routledge, 1995), p.52 and p.56.

24 As stated in 'A Note on Money and Inflation' at the start of this volume, it is hard to say exactly how much this would be today. Calculations by Georg Heinrich Paritius valued 40 livres at £3 sterling in 1707. This would make 6,000 livers around £450 at the time; See G.H. Paritius, *Cambio Mercatorio* (Regensberg: n.p., 1709).

25 M. Milevsky, *King William's Tontine: Why the Retirement Annuity of the Future Should Resemble Its Past* (Cambridge: Cambridge University Press, 2015), p.42; C. Rietsch and G. Gallais-Hamonno, 'Lorenzo Tonti', in P. Hellwege (ed.), *The Past, Present, and Future of Tontines: A Seventeenth Century Financial Product and the Development of Life Insurance* (Berlin: Duncker & Humblot, 2018), p.40; and F. Hendriks, 'Notes on the Early History of Tontines', *The Assurance Magazine, and Journal of the Institute of Actuaries*, Vol. 10, No. 4 (July, 1862), p.208.

26 D.R. Weir, 'Tontines, Public Finance, and Revolution in France and England, 1688–1789', *The Journal of Economic History,* Vol. 49, No. 1 (March, 1989), p.102.

27 The conflict had a death-toll which, proportionally, surpassed either of the twentieth century's world wars; P.H. Wilson, *The Thirty Years War: A Sourcebook* (Basingstoke: Bloomsbury, 2010), p.1.

28 R.M. Jennings and A.P. Trout, *The Tontine: From the Reign of Louis XIV to the French Revolutionary Era* (Philadelphia: University of Pennsylvania, 1982), p.4.

29 E. Clingan, *Capitalism: A Modern Economic History* (Bloomington, IN: iUniverse, 2015); and E.J. Hamilton, 'Origin and Growth of the National Debt in Western Europe', *The American Economic Review*, Vol. 37, No. 2 (1947), p.120.

30 D. Parrott, *1652: The Cardinal, the Prince, and the Crisis of the 'Fronde'* (Oxford: Oxford University Press, 2020), p.1.

31 D. Parrott, *1652: The Cardinal, the Prince, and the Crisis of the 'Fronde'* (Oxford: Oxford University Press, 2020), p.1; and R.M. Jennings and A.P. Trout, *The Tontine: From the Reign of Louis XIV to the French Revolutionary Era* (Philadelphia: University of Pennsylvania, 1982), p.4.

32 R.M. Jennings and A.P. Trout, *The Tontine: From the Reign of Louis XIV to the French Revolutionary Era* (Philadelphia: University of Pennsylvania, 1982), p.4.

33 R.M. Jennings and A.P. Trout, *The Tontine: From the Reign of Louis XIV to the French Revolutionary Era* (Philadelphia: University of Pennsylvania, 1982), p.5; in 1634 7 per cent annuities were sold which actually paid annual interest of 33–50 per cent.

34 M. Milevsky, *King William's Tontine: Why the Retirement Annuity of the Future Should Resemble Its Past* (Cambridge: Cambridge University Press, 2015), p.26.

35 K. McKeever, 'A Short History of Tontines', *Fordham Journal of Corporate and Financial Law*, Vol. 15, Issue 42, (2009), pp.494–495.

36 L. Tonti, 'Edict for the King for the Creation of the Society of the Royal Tontine' (1654), translated by Véronique Gasseau-Dryer, in S. Haberman and T.A. Sibbett (eds), *History of Actuarial Science*, Vol. 5 (of 10) (London: Routledge, 1995), p.4; Class 1, 0–7; class 2, 7–14; class 3, 14–21; class 4, 21–28; class 5, 28–35, class 6; 35–42; class 7, 42–49; class 8, 49–55; class 9, 55–63; class 10, 63 and above.

37 L. Tonti, 'Edict for the King for the Creation of the Society of the Royal Tontine' (1654), translated by Véronique Gasseau-Dryer, in S. Haberman and T.A. Sibbett (eds), *History of Actuarial Science*, Vol. 5 (of 10) (London: Routledge, 1995), p.4; and C. Rietsch and G. Gallais-Hamonno, 'Lorenzo Tonti', in P. Hellwege (ed.), *The Past, Present, and Future of Tontines: A Seventeenth Century Financial Product and the Development of Life Insurance* (Berlin: Duncker & Humblot, 2018), p.32.

38 L. Tonti, 'Edict for the King for the Creation of the Society of the Royal Tontine' (1654), translated by Véronique Gasseau-Dryer, in S. Haberman and T.A. Sibbett (eds), *History of Actuarial Science*, Vol. 5 (of 10) (London: Routledge, 1995), pp.14–15.

39 R.M. Jennings and A.P Trout, *The Tontine: From the Reign of Louis XIV to the French Revolutionary Era* (Philadelphia: University of Pennsylvania, 1982), p.6.

40 G. Gallais-Hamonno and J. Berthon, *Les emprunts tontiniers de l'Ancien Règime, un exemple d'ingènierie financière au XVIII siècle* (Paris: Sorbonne Publications, 2008), p.8; and K. McKeever, 'A Short History of Tontines', *Fordham Journal of Corporate and Financial Law* (2009), p.493.

41 D.R. Weir, 'Tontines, Public Finance, and Revolution in France and England, 1688–1789', *The Journal of Economic History,* Vol. 49, No. 1 (March, 1989), p.104; and G. Gallais-Hamonno and O. Rietsch, 'Financial Engineering in the 17th and 18th Centuries', in P. Hellwege, *The Past, Present and Future of Tontines: A Seventeenth Century Financial Product and the Development of Life Insurance* (Berlin: Duncker & Humblot, 2018), p.51.

42 See 'Correspondance Administrative sous le Régne de Louis XVI., entre le Cabinet du Roi, les Secrétaires d'Etat, &c. Recueillie et mise en ordre par G.B. Depping', Vol. 3 (Paris, 1852); cited in Hendriks, 'Notes on the Early History of Tontines', p.209.

43 C. Rietsch and G. Gallais-Hamonno, 'Lorenzo Tonti', in P. Hellwege (ed.), *The Past, Present, and Future of Tontines: A Seventeenth Century Financial Product and the Development of Life Insurance* (Berlin: Duncker & Humblot, 2018), p.35.

44 A tontine did eventually go ahead in the Languedoc region, but this was not until 1684 and was without Tonti's involvement; see C. Rietsch and G. Gallais-Hamonno, 'Lorenzo Tonti', in P. Hellwege (ed.), *The Past, Present, and Future of Tontines: A Seventeenth Century Financial Product and the Development of Life Insurance* (Berlin: Duncker & Humblot, 2018), pp.37–39.

45 C. Rietsch and G. Gallais-Hamonno, 'Lorenzo Tonti', in P. Hellwege (ed.), *The Past, Present, and Future of Tontines: A Seventeenth Century Financial Product and the Development of Life Insurance* (Berlin: Duncker & Humblot, 2018), p.43.

46 There is uncertainty as to who these two sons were. Henri and Alphonse were both in the Americas at this point. Tonti had previously stated in personal correspondence that he had 17 dependents, and it is possible he married twice.

47 C. Rietsch and G. Gallais-Hamonno, 'Lorenzo Tonti', in P. Hellwege (ed.), *The Past, Present, and Future of Tontines: A Seventeenth Century Financial Product and the Development of Life Insurance* (Berlin: Duncker & Humblot, 2018), p.44; F. Hendriks, 'Notes on the Early History of Tontines', *The Assurance Magazine, and Journal of the Institute of Actuaries*, Vol. 10, No. 4 (July, 1862), pp.205–219; and

K. McKeever, 'A Short History of Tontines', *Fordham Journal of Corporate and Financial Law* (2009), p.493.

48 A. Hald, *A History of Probability and Statistics and Their Applications before 1750* (Hoboken, NJ: Wiley, 1990), p.120.

49 M. Sunnqvist, 'Tontines in Scandinavia', in P. Hellwege (ed.), *The Past, Present and Future of Tontines: A Seventeenth Century Financial Product and the Development of Life Insurance* (Berlin: Duncker & Humblot, 2018), p.159.

50 M. Sunnqvist, 'Tontines in Scandinavia', in P. Hellwege (ed.), *The Past, Present and Future of Tontines: A Seventeenth Century Financial Product and the Development of Life Insurance* (Berlin: Duncker & Humblot, 2018), p.160.

51 A. Hald, *A History of Probability and Statistics and Their Applications before 1750* (Hoboken, NJ: Wiley, 1990), p.120.

52 M. Sunnqvist, 'Tontines in Scandinavia', in P. Hellwege (ed.), *The Past, Present and Future of Tontines: A Seventeenth Century Financial Product and the Development of Life Insurance* (Berlin: Duncker & Humblot, 2018), p.161.

53 P. Hellwege, *A History of Tontines in Germany: From a Multi-purpose Financial Product to a Single-purpose Pension Product* (Berlin: Duncker & Humblot, 2018), pp.26–27.

54 P. Hellwege, 'Tontines in German-speaking Territories', in P. Hellwege (ed.), *The Past, Present, Future of Tontines: A Seventeenth Century Financial Product and the Development of Life Insurance* (Berlin: Duncker & Humblot, 2018), p.169.

55 P. Hellwege, *A History of Tontines in Germany: From a Multi-purpose Financial Product to a Single-purpose Pension Product* (Berlin: Duncker & Humblot, 2018), pp.38–40.

56 P. Hellwege, *A History of Tontines in Germany: From a Multi-purpose Financial Product to a Single-purpose Pension Product* (Berlin: Duncker & Humblot, 2018), pp.40–41.

57 P. Hellwege, *A History of Tontines in Germany: From a Multi-purpose Financial Product to a Single-purpose Pension Product* (Berlin: Duncker & Humblot, 2018), p.42.

58 P. Hellwege, *A History of Tontines in Germany: From a Multi-purpose Financial Product to a Single-purpose Pension Product* (Berlin: Duncker & Humblot, 2018), p.170.

59 J. Atack and L. Neal, *The Origins and Development of Financial Markets* (Cambridge: Cambridge University Press, 2009), pp.90–91.

60 B. Sirks, 'Tontines in the Dutch Republic and the Early Kingdom (1670–1869)', in P. Hellwege (ed.), *The Past, Present, and Future of Tontines: A Seventeenth Century Financial Product and the Development of Life Insurance* (Berlin: Duncker & Humblot, 2018), p.124; and K. McKeever, 'A Short History of Tontines', *Fordham Journal of Corporate and Financial Law* (2009), p.493.

61 J. Atack and L. Neal, *The Origins and Development of Financial Markets* (Cambridge: Cambridge University Press, 2009), p.91.

62 J. Atack and L. Neal, *The Origins and Development of Financial Markets* (Cambridge: Cambridge University Press, 2009), pp.91–92.

63 J. Atack and L. Neal, *The Origins and Development of Financial Markets* (Cambridge: Cambridge University Press, 2009), p.91; and K. McKeever, 'A Short History of Tontines', *Fordham Journal of Corporate and Financial Law* (2009), p.493.

64 J. Atack and L. Neal, *The Origins and Development of Financial Markets* (Cambridge: Cambridge University Press, 2009), p.9.

65 P.G.M. Dickson, *The Financial Revolution in England: A Study in the Development of Public Credit, 1688–1756* (London: Routledge, 1993), p.41.

66 The only differences were class 8, which was 49–56, and class 9, 56–63, rather than Tonti's 49–55 and 55–63.

67 P. Cardonnel, *Proposals for Increase of Wealth by Subscriptions of Money, according to the Several Particualrs Herein Mentions*, 2nd edn (London: Nathanael Brooke, 1675), pp.1–3.

68 *Some Considerations upon the Proposals Approved of by the City of London for Subscriptions on Lives, Wherein Are Some Observations and Conjectures upon the East India Company and Banker, in Hendriks*, 'Notes on the Early History of Tontines', Appendix B, pp.213–219.
69 R.M. Jennings and A.P Trout, *The Tontine: From the Reign of Louis XIV to the French Revolutionary Era* (Philadelphia: University of Pennsylvania, 1982), p.16.
70 R.M. Jennings and A.P Trout, *The Tontine: From the Reign of Louis XIV to the French Revolutionary Era* (Philadelphia: University of Pennsylvania, 1982), p.16.
71 R.M. Jennings and A.P Trout, *The Tontine: From the Reign of Louis XIV to the French Revolutionary Era* (Philadelphia: University of Pennsylvania, 1982), pp.16–17.
72 M. Milevsky, *King William's Tontine: Why the Retirement Annuity of the Future Should Resemble Its Past* (Cambridge: Cambridge University Press, 2015), p.98.
73 G. Gallais-Hamonno and O. Rietsch, 'Financial Engineering in the 17th and 18th Centuries', in P. Hellwege, *The Past, Present and Future of Tontines: A Seventeenth Century Financial Product and the Development of Life Insurance* (Berlin: Duncker & Humblot, 2018), p.54.
74 R.M. Jennings and A.P Trout, *The Tontine: From the Reign of Louis XIV to the French Revolutionary Era* (Philadelphia: University of Pennsylvania, 1982), p.21.
75 G. Gallais-Hamonno and O. Rietsch, 'Financial Engineering in the 17th and 18th Centuries', in P. Hellwege, *The Past, Present and Future of Tontines: A Seventeenth Century Financial Product and the Development of Life Insurance* (Berlin: Duncker & Humblot, 2018), p.53.
76 R.M. Jennings, D.F. Swanson and A.P. Trout, 'Alexander Hamilton's Tontine Proposal', *The William and Mary Quarterly*, Vol. 45, No. 1 (1988), p.108.
77 G. Gallais-Hamonno and O. Rietsch, 'Financial Engineering in the 17th and 18th Centuries', in P. Hellwege, *The Past, Present and Future of Tontines: A Seventeenth Century Financial Product and the Development of Life Insurance* (Berlin: Duncker & Humblot, 2018), p.66.
78 1689 collected 18.4 per cent, whilst 1696 did a little better at 20.46 per cent; G. Gallais-Hamonno and O. Rietsch, 'Financial Engineering in the 17th and 18th Centuries', in P. Hellwege, *The Past, Present and Future of Tontines: A Seventeenth Century Financial Product and the Development of Life Insurance* (Berlin: Duncker & Humblot, 2018); see D.R. Weir, 'Tontines, Public Finance, and Revolution in France and England, 1688–1789', *The Journal of Economic History*, Vol. 49, No. 1 (March, 1989) , p.105; and R.M. Jennings and A.P Trout, *The Tontine: From the Reign of Louis XIV to the French Revolutionary Era* (Philadelphia: University of Pennsylvania, 1982), p.19.
79 For an excellent and accessible piece of scholarship on the revolution, and the events which predated and followed it, see T. Harris, *Revolution: The Great Crisis of the British Monarchy, 1685–1720* (London: Penguin Group, 2007).
80 A. McDiarmid, *Credit, Capital, and Currency: The Scottish Financial Revolution, 1690–1727* (Abingdon: Routledge, 2023), p.10.
81 G. Gallais-Hamonno and O. Rietsch, 'Financial Engineering in the 17th and 18th Centuries', in P. Hellwege, *The Past, Present and Future of Tontines: A Seventeenth Century Financial Product and the Development of Life Insurance* (Berlin: Duncker & Humblot, 2018), p.51.
82 G. Gallais-Hamonno and O. Rietsch, 'Financial Engineering in the 17th and 18th Centuries', in P. Hellwege, *The Past, Present and Future of Tontines: A Seventeenth Century Financial Product and the Development of Life Insurance* (Berlin: Duncker & Humblot, 2018), p.51.
83 M. Milevsky, *King William's Tontine: Why the Retirement Annuity of the Future Should Resemble Its Past* (Cambridge: Cambridge University Press, 2015), pp.37–40.

84 P.G.M. Dickson, *The Financial Revolution in England: A Study in the Development of Public Credit, 1688–1756* (London: Routledge, 1993); Dickson states 'It seems probable … though there is no direct evidence, that Paterson was the author of the proposal for a tontine loan which the commons accepted in December 1692'.
85 R.M. Jennings, D.F. Swanson and A.P. Trout, 'Alexander Hamilton's Tontine Proposal', *The William and Mary Quarterly*, Vol. 45, No. 1 (1988), p.109.
86 M. Milevsky, *King William's Tontine: Why the Retirement Annuity of the Future Should Resemble Its Past* (Cambridge: Cambridge University Press, 2015), p.56; and G. Gallais-Hamonno and O. Rietsch, 'Financial Engineering in the 17th and 18th Centuries', in P. Hellwege, *The Past, Present and Future of Tontines: A Seventeenth Century Financial Product and the Development of Life Insurance* (Berlin: Duncker & Humblot, 2018), p.54.
87 E. Halley, 'An Estimate of the Degrees of the Mortality of Mankind, Drawn from Curious Tables of the Births and Funerals at the City of Breslaw, with an Attempt to Ascertain the Price of Annuities upon Lives', in *Philosophical Transactions of the Royal Society*, Vol.17, Issue 196, (London, 1693), pp.596-610; and M. Milevsky, *King William's Tontine: Why the Retirement Annuity of the Future Should Resemble Its Past* (Cambridge: Cambridge University Press, 2015), pp.64–66.
88 M. Milevsky, *King William's Tontine: Why the Retirement Annuity of the Future Should Resemble Its Past* (Cambridge: Cambridge University Press, 2015), pp.61–62.
89 D.R. Weir, 'Tontines, Public Finance, and Revolution in France and England, 1688–1789', *The Journal of Economic History,* Vol. 49, No. 1 (March, 1989), p.105.
90 M. Milevsky, *King William's Tontine: Why the Retirement Annuity of the Future Should Resemble Its Past* (Cambridge: Cambridge University Press, 2015), 'Appendix A: The List of Nominees', pp.201–225.
91 M. Milevsky, *King William's Tontine: Why the Retirement Annuity of the Future Should Resemble Its Past* (Cambridge: Cambridge University Press, 2015), 'Appendix A: The List of Nominees', p.44.

Bibliography

Primary Sources

Cardonnel, P., *Proposals for Increase of Wealth by Subscriptions of Money, according to the Several Particualrs Herein Mentions*, 2nd edn (London: Nathanael Brooke, 1675).

Halley, E., 'An Estimate of the Degrees of the Mortality of Mankind, Drawn from Curious Tables of the Births and Funerals at the City of Breslaw, with an Attempt to Ascertain the Price of Annuities upon Lives', *Philosophical Transactions of the Royal Society*, Vol.17, Issue 196, (London, 1693), pp.596–610 .

Paritius, G.H., *Cambio Mercatorio* (Regensberg: n.p., 1709).

Stevenson, R.L. and Osbourne, L., *The Wrong Box* (London; Longmans, Green & Co., 1889).

Tonti, H., *Dernieres Decouvertes dans L'Amerique Septentrionale de M. De La Sale* (Paris: Jean Guignard, 1697).

Tonti, L., 'Edict for the King for the Creation of the Society of the Royal Tontine' (1653) (V. Gasseau-Dryer, Trans.), reprinted in S. Haberman and T.A. Sibbett (eds.), *History of Actuarial Science* (Vol. 5, p.4) (London: Routledge, 1995).

Books

Atack, J. and Neal, L., *The Origins and Development of Financial Markets and Institutions: From the Seventeenth Century to the Present* (Cambridge: Cambridge University Press, 2009).

Catherwood, M.H., *The Story of Tonty* (Chicago: A. C. McClurg and Company, 1890).

Clingan, E., *Capitalism: A Modern Economic History* (Bloomington, IN: iUniverse, 2015).

Delicato, A., *Italians in Detroit* (Chicago: Arcadia Publishing, 2005).

Dickson, P.G.M., *The Financial Revolution in England: A Study in the Development of Public Credit, 1688–1756* (London: Routledge, 1993).

Gallais-Hamonno, G. and Berthon, J., *Les emprunts tontiniers de l'Ancien Règime, un exemple d'ingènierie financière au XVIII siècle* (Paris: Sorbonne Publications, 2008).

Hald, A., *A History of Probability and Statistics and their Applications before* 1750 (Hoboken, NJ: Wiley, 1990).

Harris, T., *Revolution: The Great Crisis of the British Monarchy, 1685–1720* (London: Penguin Group, 2007).

Hellwege, P., *A History of Tontines in Germany: From a Multi-purpose Financial Product to a Single-purpose Pension Product* (Berlin: Duncker & Humblot, 2018).

Jennings, R.M. and Trout, A.P., *The Tontine: From the Reign of Louis XIV to the French Revolutionary Era* (Philadelphia: University of Pennsylvania, 1982).

Legler, H.E., *The Man with the Iron Hand Chevalier Henry de Tonty's Exploits in the Valley of the Mississippi* (Milwaukee: n.p., 1896).

McDiarmid, A., *Credit, Capital, and Currency: The Scottish Financial Revolution, 1690–1727* (Abingdon: Routledge, 2023).

Michie, R.C., *The London Stock Exchange: A History* (Oxford: Oxford University Press, 1999).

Milevsky, M., *King William's Tontine: Why the Retirement Annuity of the Future Should Resemble Its Past* (Cambridge: Cambridge University Press, 2015).

Murphy, A., *The Origins of English Financial Markets: Investment and Speculation before the South Sea Bubble* (Cambridge: Cambridge University Press, 2009).

Murphy, E.R., *Henry de Tonty: Fur Trader of the Mississippi* (Baltimore: Johns Hopkins Press, 1941).

Parrott, D., *1652: The Cardinal, the Prince, and the Crisis of the 'Fronde'* (Oxford: Oxford University Press, 2020).

Stigler, S., *Statistics on the Table: The History of Statistical Concepts and Methods* (Boston: Harvard University Press, 2002).

Treasure, G., *Mazarin: The Crisis of Absolutism in France* (London: Routledge, 1995).

Wilson, P.H., *The Thirty Years War: A Sourcebook* (Basingstoke: Bloomsbury, 2010).

Edited Collection and Journal Articles

Fortunati, M. 'Tontines in Italy', in Hellwege, P. (ed.), *The Past, Present, and Future of Tontines: A Seventeenth Century Financial Product and the Development of Life Insurance* (Berlin: Duncker & Humblot, 2018), pp.203–228.

Gallais-Hamonno, G. and Rietsch, O., 'Financial Engineering in the 17th and 18th Centuries', in Hellwege, P. (ed.), *The Past, Present, and Future of Tontines: A Seventeenth Century Financial Product and the Development of Life Insurance* (Berlin: Duncker & Humblot, 2018), pp.49–78.

Hamilton, E.J., 'Origin and Growth of the National Debt in Western Europe', *The American Economic Review*, Vol. 37, No. 2 (1947), pp.118–130.

Hendriks, F., 'Notes on the Early History of Tontines', *The Assurance Magazine, and Journal of the Institute of Actuaries*, Vol. 10, No. 4 (1862), pp.205–219.

Higginbotham, J., 'Henri de Tonti's Mission to the Chickasaw, 1702', *Louisiana History*, Vol. 19 (1978), pp.285–296.

Jennings, R.M., Swanson, D.F. and Trout, A.P., 'Alexander Hamilton's Tontine Proposal', *The William and Mary Quarterly*, Vol. 45, No. 1 (1988), pp.107–115.

Jennings, R.M. and Trout, A.P., 'The Tontine Re-examined: A Modest Proposal to Reduce the National Debt', *Economy and History*, Vol. 17, No. 1 (1974), pp.106–115.

McKeever, K., 'A Short History of Tontines', *Fordham Journal of Corporate and Financial Law*, Vol. 15, Issue 42, (2009), pp.491–521.

McKeever, K., 'Tontines in Portugal – Nicholas Bourey's Paleo-Tontine of 1641', in Hellwege, P. (ed.), *The Past, Present, and Future of Tontines: A Seventeenth Century Financial Product and the Development of Life Insurance* (Berlin: Duncker & Humblot, 2018), pp.191–201.

Rietsch, C. and Gallais-Hamonno, G., 'Lorenzo Tonti', in Hellwege, P. (ed.), *The Past, Present, and Future of Tontines: A Seventeenth Century Financial Product and the Development of Life Insurance* (Berlin: Duncker & Humblot, 2018), pp.19–47.

Sirks, B., 'Tontines in the Dutch Republic and the Early Kingdom (1670–1869)', in Hellwege, P. (ed.), *The Past, Present, and Future of Tontines: A Seventeenth Century Financial Product and the Development of Life Insurance* (Berlin: Duncker & Humblot, 2018), pp.121–142.

Sunnqvist, M., 'Tontines in Scandinavia', in Hellwege, P. (ed.), *The Past, Present, and Future of Tontines: A Seventeenth Century Financial Product and the Development of Life Insurance* (Berlin: Duncker & Humblot, 2018), pp.153–166.

Weir, D.R., 'Tontines, Public Finance, and Revolution in France and England, 1688–1789', *The Journal of Economic History*, Vol. 49, No. 1 (1989), pp.95–126.

3 Public Tontines in the Eighteenth Century

It would be fair to say that the large-scale government tontines of the late seventeenth century were not a success. As the reader will recall from the last chapter, the first French tontine of 1689 had stalled at around 3.6 million of its intended 19.6 million livres target, while the 1696 follow-up raised just over 2.9 million of the lower target of 14 million livres. This poor performance was echoed in the first English tontine of 1693, which reached just 10.8 per cent of its £1 million target.[1] Despite this disappointing start, French and English governments persisted with the scheme for much of the eighteenth century. For the French this meant the implementation of new tontines was carried out at speed, with eight schemes established between 1709 and 1759. In England the pace was slower. After the inaugural English tontine of 1693, the next attempt was not until 1757, by which time the plan was carried out by the British, rather than English, government.[2] Due to a lack of subscriptions, however, the 1757 tontine was cancelled and replaced with an offer of life annuities and government consols. The follow-up to the tontine of 1693 was therefore not established until 1765.[3] There was then one final British tontine in 1789. Aside from France and England, there were also three very successful tontines offered by the Irish government during the 1770s.

Now, you may be asking yourself, 'what did these governments spend the tontine money on?' The short answer was (usually) war; what else? Every public tontine organised by French or English/British governments, except the British scheme of 1789, appeared at a time when budgets were being stretched due to the cost of war; sometimes against one another.[4] While the Irish tontines of 1773, 1775, and 1777 coincided with the American War of Independence (1775–1783), they appear to have been driven by a shortfall in government funding rather than the North American war.

This chapter will cover this boom in publicly administered tontines across the eighteenth century. It will provide a comparison of those which were offered in France and in Britain, and an overview of the tontines established in Ireland. The chapter will also consider public tontines offered in other areas of Europe and will conclude with a short section on a tontine proposed for the United States, by Alexander Hamilton, the first Secretary of the Treasury for the young republic.

DOI: 10.4324/9781003491002-3

A Tale of Two Tontines: The Scheme in Eighteenth-century France and Britain

While the duo of seventeenth-century French tontines had faltered at around 20 per cent of their intended total, those which emerged during the next century were far more successful. The eight tontines issued between 1709 and 1759 collected 107.5 per cent of their intended total on average. Even the most poorly performing French tontine of the eighteenth century, that of 1733, still managed to collect 11.1 million of the 12 million livres it sought to raise.[5] There was therefore a significant appetite among investors for French tontines at this time.

The tontine of 1709 was conceived in the midst of the War of the Spanish Succession (1701–1714). The seeds of the conflict had been sown in late 1700, when Charles II, the sickly Spanish king, died at the age of 39 with no direct heir. Prior to his passing, Charles had nominated Philip of Anjou, the grandson of French king, Louis XIV, to take the throne after his death. Concerned as to what this would mean for the balance of power on the continent, a bloc of European states, known as the Grand Alliance, coalesced behind a rival to the Spanish throne, Holy Roman Emperor, Charles VI.[6] The scheme which emerged at this time as a method of partly funding the conflict was different from earlier French tontines and combined a tontine with *perpetual rentes*.[7] The *rentes* were government bonds which did not mature but rather paid a regular ongoing dividend and had been declining in popularity due to slow and irregular interest payments. As previous French tontines had met with limited success, it was hoped that a combination of the two might excite more interest from investors.[8]

The scheme was intended to raise a sum of 6 million livres, split equally between *rentes* and the tontine, through the sale of shares priced at 600 livres each; twice the price of earlier tontine shares. In return, subscribers would receive an initial annuity of 50 livres, comprised of 30 livres from the *rentes* and the remainder, which would increase with the benefit of survivorship, from the tontine. This meant that should a nominee die, then all would not be lost, with subscribers and their heirs continuing to receive the 30 livres tied to the *rentes*.[9]

In the end the scheme was a bit of a mixed success. Responding to wary investors, the government sought to boost the attractiveness of the investment by accepting its own notes as part-payment for the shares. These largely took the form of notes that had been issued to cover the subsistence of French troops and were likely paper that no one else would accept.[10] The offer worked, and despite subscription to the classes being uneven, the tontine raised 2.96 million of its 3 million livre target.[11] The French government later reneged on the deal, however, reducing the interest paid on the *rentes* from five to four per cent in 1713 and separating this from the tontine element of the scheme.[12]

Following the 1709 tontine, there was a gap of almost a quarter of a century before the French government ran another scheme. The 1733 tontine was made up of seven classes, and with over 14,000 nominees appears to have been the largest scheme offered anywhere up to that date. This was quickly followed in 1734 by a slightly smaller offering with 12,653 nominees, spread across 15 classes with 175 subdivisions.[13] Together these raised close to 27.5 million livres.[14] During the 1740s there was then a flurry of French tontine activity. This included two fully subscribed schemes in 1743, raising a combined total of 12.6 million livres; a fully subscribed tontine in 1744 which raised 9 million livres; and one in 1745 which missed it's 9 million livres target by just 1,800 livres. The final French government tontine, by far the largest scheme ever operated in France (and likely anywhere else), consisted of just short of 50,000 nominees and surpassed its 30 million livres target by more than 16 million livres, was then offered in 1759.[15]

In England, meanwhile, the tontine was not in such rude health. There the scheme only every became a minor revenue-raising tool, with the second attempt to establish a tontine not occurring until 1757. This was more developed than the scheme of 1693 with its one nominee pool, and instead divided nominees into five separate classes. Each class was offered a different starting interest rate, which increased in line with the age of the nominees, for a subscription price of £100. It was hoped that £2.5 million would be raised, but in the face of a poor public response it yielded just over £300,000 and was subsequently cancelled. As an alternative the British parliament passed a bill to raise £3 million through a combination of government bonds and life annuities.[16] Those who had already invested in the tontine were switched to the new offer.

One would have thought that with such little public interest in tontines, the British government would have shelved the scheme, yet just eight years later in 1765 a new tontine was offered. This was part of a financial inducement attached to a larger government loan, and despite the scheme raising just £18,000 of the targeted £300,000, and with only 900 nominees grouped together in one class, it went ahead.[17]

24 years then passed until the British government offered its next and final tontine in 1789. This was the best subscribed example undertaken there and raised over £429,000 of its £1 million target.[18] It was the also first English/British tontine with more than one class to become operational, separating its 3,495 nominees into 6 age groups; 0–19; 20–29; 30–39; 40–49; 50–59; and 60 and upwards. Each class was offered a different initial annuity rate, increasing incrementally from just over four per cent for the youngest group of nominees, up to just shy of six per cent for the oldest.[19] While the share price remained at £100, organisers introduced an innovation to the scheme at this point, capping the amount that could be paid in annuities to £1,000 per subscription; presumably to reduce the government's future liabilities. This meant that subscribers would not receive the huge returns seen in some other schemes, but could still, in theory, collect an excellent 900 per cent return on their investment per year.

A comparison of French and English/British tontines demonstrates that the French were far more effective at bringing money into government coffers. In part, this was due to structural problems in English/British tontines. These schemes generally offered a return tied to interest at market rates, while the French offered a higher level of interest; this was especially true when it came to older nominees.[20] The French also priced their shares cheaper, widening the potential investor pool.[21] A subscription to the French 1689 tontine cost 300 livres, while the English scheme of 1693 priced its subscriptions at £100 each; a price that continued for eighteenth-century British tontines. While it is difficult to discern an exact exchange rate in 1693, Milevsky, using the figures provided by Jennings and Trout, has calculated 'the currency-adjusted cost of a French tontine share was approximately £12.5'. This may be underestimating the cost a little, however, for if we use Paritius' exchange rates from 1709, a 300 livres share in a French tontine equated to around £22.[22] As was covered in the last chapter, this does not mean that French tontines were for all members of French society, but it certainly widened participation far more than the English/British equivalent.[23]

While the British tontine of 1789 was the most successful offered by that government, and despite the French having refined a popular model for investors, public tontines began to wane in popularity as the eighteenth century drew to a close. This was in part due to the difficulty in administering such a complex system. The French had put in place more structures to manage the process, operating a regulatory model in which the largest tontine shareholders elected administrators from among themselves to manage the scheme. This gave French administrators an interest in making sure the tontine was properly run and differed from English/British and Irish schemes poorly managed by the Treasury, a body with no immediate interest in making sure tontines were managed accordingly.[24] Within the administrative limitations of the eighteenth century, these large national tontines were complicated and potentially problematic regardless of how they were governed, but poor management certainly did not help. There was also a sense of disillusionment among investors. They had after all been promised significant returns on their investment, and while a limited number saw exceptional returns, for many these had been disappointing.

Governments had also begun to question the financial soundness of borrowing via tontine. Doing so tied the state to long-term debt and by the second half of the eighteenth century represented an expensive form of borrowing. The French were first to come to this realisation, banning all future government tontines in 1763.[25] In Britain, the government persisted a little longer with the scheme before it was abandoned. There, tontines had met with limited success and had always been a minor revenue-raising tool. It was much more fiscally sound for the government to enter into loan agreements with institutions like the Bank of England or East India Company, from which it could borrow significant sums at low interest. From the 1750s there was also the emergence of three per cent consols, a British government-issued annuity, which later reduced the attractiveness of the tontine.[26] Consequently, the British Tontine of 1789 marked the country's last large-scale public tontine.

Irish Tontines of the 1770s

By the time the first Irish government tontine was offered in 1773, organisers could look back on schemes offered elsewhere for inspiration. The result was a tontine that fell somewhere between those which operated in Britain and their French counterparts. Each of the three Irish tontines (1773, 1775, and 1777) operated with three classes; class 1, 40-years-old and above; class 2, 20–39; and class 3, 0–19. This was at a time when English/British tontines had not yet operated separate age classes for nominees but was still a long way off the complexity of French schemes, where nominees could be separated into up to 15 classes and hundreds of subdivisions. Yet, while Irish tontines lacked the actuarial nuance of their French counterparts, they certainly mirrored their popularity, with all three fully subscribed and raising a combined total of IR£740,000.[27]

Like English/British tontines, the first Irish tontine priced shares at £100 each (as did subsequent offerings). To limit the government's financial commitments, organisers decided to cap the annuity amount that could be paid and ruled that the annuity could not exceed the initial subscription price.[28] This would stop subscribers making huge returns but still offered up to £100 per year for an initial £100 investment.[29] This may have affected investor interest, because while the tontine would eventually be fully subscribed, the uptake of subscriptions was initially slow. This led the Irish government, in a manner similar to its British counterpart before it, to undermine the tontine offer by suggesting that it would be transferred into a lottery if subscription numbers proved inadequate.[30] The government should not have worried, and despite an unhurried start, investors eventually proved eager to put their money into Irish tontines.[31]

That there was an 80-year gap between the first English and Irish tontines does not mean that there was not an awareness of the scheme in Ireland. Dating back to the English tontine of 1693, there had been limited Irish involvement, with two Irish nominees noted in the subscription list.[32] More substantial evidence of a wider knowledge of the tontine in the country is supported by the inclusion of several tontine-related stories in the Irish press in the years prior to 1773. News of tontines in France, Austria, England, and Scotland were regularly communicated to Irish readers.[33] These included reports in *The Belfast Newsletter* on the progress of a proposed French tontine in 1762; issues around low take-up of subscriptions affecting the English tontine of 1765; and plans by the British East India Company to establish a tontine in 1769.[34] Stories detailed how tontines were being operated, the sums which were being raised, and often the specifics of the schemes' rates of return. Letters pages in the Irish press also demonstrated that a section of its readership was fully engaged with the tontine and finance more widely. Authored under *noms de plume* such as 'Numscull' and 'Plain Truth', readers' letters provided analysis of the financial aspects of the tontine and show a good understanding of the scheme.[35] Ireland's investing class could therefore not have failed to be aware of the tontine much earlier than 1773.

When it came to the Irish government tontines, contemporary newspapers illustrate that there was significant interest around these. A report in *The Freeman's Journal*, a leading nationalist newspaper, covered the parliamentary debate on the first tontine in late November 1773.[36] The idea was raised by Irish Attorney General, Philip Tisdale, who promoted it as a method of plugging a government funding deficit. Tisdale's plan was met with resistance from some quarters. Sir William Mayne, a British merchant and the member of parliament for Carysfort, County Wicklow, for example, stated that he could not support the scheme 'on account of its novelty', and instead favoured the issuance of Exchequer Bills to provide the required funding; a suggestion that was roundly rejected.[37] Other parliamentary representatives feared that the tontine was too close in nature to a lottery, which was viewed as the 'last resort of a weak government'; while others were concerned over the taxes which would be levied to pay the tontine annuities. The representative for County Mayo, Sir Charles Bingham, meanwhile, dismissed it as a 'French or Italian scheme' unfit for 'a free government'.[38] After reading the press coverage, a betting man may have judged the odds of the bill getting through parliament as slim to none. Yet, despite being initially rejected, it was passed by the House in December 1773.

Even in the face of some trepidation from Irish parliamentarians, the Irish government tontines of the 1770s were a success.[39] All three were fully subscribed and brought significant funds into government coffers. Yet, it remained an expensive form of borrowing, and despite its popularity, the Irish government did not offer another after 1777. The long-term nature of the tontine meant, however, that successive Irish governments were tied to annuities payments until the last tontine nominee died almost a century later, in 1870.

Immortal Nominees? A Formula for the Irish Tontine of 1777

While there was a large element of luck in selecting a tontine nominee, there were steps that subscribers could take to give themselves the best chance of success. One appears to have been by selecting a female nominee. Over the course of the three Irish government tontines, 3,384 nominees were selected in total, of which 58 per cent were female.[40] This was a selection that certainly paid off, with a report compiled for the British government in 1860 on tontines and annuities, stating that 120 female nominees from the three tontines were still alive compared to 60 men.[41] A second factor was to choose a young nominee who provided the opportunity for long-term, high returns. Subscribers to the Irish tontines largely followed this pattern, with nominees leaning towards the more youthful, with the bulk of them being under the age of 21. There was one group of investors in the Irish tontine of 1777 that applied both of these stipulations to nominee selection, and indeed went even further in how they refined their choices, to great financial gain.

The majority of investment in the 1777 tontine came from outside of the country, with Irish investors representing just 16 per cent of the total.[42] As one would expect, English investment had been commonplace since the first Irish tontine, and in 1777 accounted for 42 per cent of all subscriptions.[43] A more distant source of investment came from the Swiss city of Geneva, from where a third of all 1777 subscriptions were bought.[44]

Included within the Genevan investors was a consortium headed by a group of bankers that were well-versed in investing in this type of scheme and which had conceived a formula for selecting nominees with the longest life expectancy; the Holy Grail for anyone investing in life contingent instruments of this type. The formula, which was devised in collaboration with medical and mortality experts, stipulated that the nominees should generally be female, aged between five and seven, and, crucially, have survived smallpox. The consortium had previously invested in French life annuities, applying their formula for nominee selection. This was met with such success that one group of nominees became known as the 'trente demoiselles de Geneve' (the 30 immortals of Geneva), due to their longevity.[45]

In 1777, the Genevan bankers applied their tried and tested formula to the Irish tontine, buying up £60,000 in subscriptions. These were secured against 50 lives, with many of the same names which appeared on the French annuities also evident in the Irish tontine's nominee list.[46] The formula again worked well, and by 1828, 51 years from the commencement of the tontine, 37 of the 50 nominees were still alive. Calculations undertaken by Casey Rothschild on investment in the 1777 tontine have demonstrated that the prudent selection of lives by Genevan bankers 'was able to improve the survival probability of nominees by as much as 50% over a 55-year period'.[47] Investing through a syndicate also spread the risk and meant that investors shared in a block of lives, so if one nominee died, the annuity may change, but it would not cease altogether.[48] As much as the tontine could be a lottery, this example by Genevan investors demonstrated a method of investment which spread the risk and turned the odds in their favour.

Other European Public Tontines

Aside from the offerings of the French, British and Irish governments, several other public tontines emerged across Europe during the eighteenth century. These were proposed and organised by municipality councils, regional governments, and local nobility to raise revenue. It should be noted, however, that the fragmentary nature of historical records related to many of these tontines frequently obscures whether proposed schemes were ever actualised.

As was the case in France and Britain, tontines in other European regions often appeared at times of war. This included an unsuccessful attempt in 1706 by Victor Amadeus II, head of the House of Savoy and a member of the Grand Alliance, to raise money to help finance the region's involvement in the War of the Spanish Succession. And another in 1733, possibly also with the involvement of Victor, who had ascended to the throne of Sardinia in 1720 before abdicating in 1730, to provide funding for the War of the Polish Succession (1733–1735). Like the earlier attempt this also failed.[49] Meanwhile in Prussia, Henrich von Bruhl, first minister in the province of Saxony had more success when he established a tontine in 1748. The scheme aimed to raise 1,050,000 thalers through the sale of 5,250 shares, priced at 200 thalers each, and was directed at covering the costs that the region had incurred during the first two Silesian Wars (1740–1742 and 1744–1745). Interestingly, the project was apparently proposed by Scotsman, Alexander Mackphaill. Unfortunately, information on Mackphaill is scarce. What we do know is that his career followed a path some might cynically call 'traditional' for his field, in that after working in the financial sector, he spent time in jail.[50]

Quite separate from covering the costs of war, the tontine also emerged in parts of Europe as a way to to fund civic improvements and support the costs of local government. Scotland for example, was never the site of a large public tontine (the reasons for which will be covered in the next chapter), but the earliest example of the scheme in the country appears to have been a 1772 plan by the Edinburgh Corporation (the city's council) for a public tontine.[51] The scheme aimed to raise £20,000 to cover the debts then accumulated by the city, but does not appear to have become operational.[52] A further proposal for a large public tontine in Edinburgh emerged in 1836. This aimed to raise £300,000, with organisers intending to secure an act of parliament to confirm the 'security of the tontine'.[53] While the scheme did not go ahead, this was as close as Scotland came to a government-backed tontine.

In German territories the tontine was only very occasionally touted as a method of funding civic building projects. Berlin's local government, for example, sought to finance the building of a new cathedral in 1747 through a tontine. The proposal was straightforward and aimed to raise 30,000 thalers through the sale of 300 subscriptions with only one class of nominee.[54] While work on the new cathedral began at this time, it is unclear if this was funded by tontine or by some other means. Later in 1788, a tontine was established in Prussia to finance road building in the region. The scheme was only open to Prussian nationals over 45 years of age, with subscribers required to invest a minimum of 500 thalers and a maximum of 2,000.[55] Tontines of this sort, and indeed in general, were not common German and German-speaking territories.

In Italy, meanwhile, there was an unsuccessful attempt to raise 16 million lire via tontine in Bologna in 1762 to cover the cost of installing street lighting in the city, as was becoming popular across Europe at the time.[56] The city of Turin had more success with the establishment of the *Cassa de' censi, prestiti ed annualità* in 1795. The institution, which was part lottery and part tontine, proved to be incredibly popular, quickly selling 362,800 tickets priced at 10 lire each.[57] Despite the initial success, the Cassa was forced to temporarily halt its business in the early 1800s. It then reopened, before permanently closing in 1847.[58]

Finally, the reader will remember from the previous chapter that Denmark had been an early adopter of the tontine, with an unsuccessful attempt in 1653.[59] Another failed attempt was made in 1694, before the country's first public tontine was established more than 50 years later.[60] This was in 1747, when the Danish state raised 100,000 rigsdaler through the sale of 1,000 tontine shares priced at 100 rigsdaler each. So successful was the scheme that demand outstripped supply, and a second tontine was established in 1757. The second scheme also priced shares at 100 rigsdaler each but provided the innovation of offering 2,400 quarter-shares. Overall, the second scheme proved to be less popular than the first, with 190,750 of the 300,000 rigsdaler target being subscribed.[61]

A Short Note on Alexander Hamilton's Tontine

When it comes to the eighteenth-century history of government tontines in the United States there is admittedly little to report. In part this may be due to the newness of the territory as an independent country, but even prior to 1776 neither France nor Britain had chosen to establish a tontine in their North American territories. There was, however, one notable proposal by Alexander Hamilton for an American tontine in 1790.

Before Hamilton was the star of a hit Broadway Hip Hop musical, he was one of the United States of America's Founding Fathers, and between 1789 and 1795 he was the country's first Secretary to the Treasury. In office, Hamilton always had one eye on England. He drew his inspiration for the Bank of the United States, formed in 1790, from the Bank of England, and his sinking fund of 1789 from British prime minister, William Pitt's, £1 million fund of three years earlier.[62] He also noticed the relative success of the 1789 British Tontine in bringing in almost half a million pounds in subscriptions. Inspired by this, Hamilton proposed a similar scheme to the US congress.

In January 1790, he produced measures designed to support public credit in the country. These included a plan to manage the debts which had been incurred in fighting the American War of Independence. Comprised of foreign, domestic, and state debts, including all associated interest, Hamilton estimated this to be $54 million at the time; this was, however, well short of the real cost, which was in excess of $75 million by 1791.[63] The plan had three main elements; (1) the conversion of high interest old debt for new lower interest instruments; (2) the funding of debt by ringfencing revenue from specific taxes for paying the interest on debt; and (3) establishing a sinking fund drawn from post office profits.[64] The tontine aspect of the plan was tied to the first element, the conversion of old debt to new.[65] Holders of old debt, which at that point paid an interest of 5.8 per cent, would be asked to trade this in for a new instrument paying 4 per cent, the tontine element was to be added as a sweetener to this initially unappealing looking offer.[66]

Hamilton's tontine proposal was largely modelled on the British scheme, with Donald Watson and Andrew Trout noticing that the terms of the proposal bore 'a remarkable similarity to those offered in 1789 by the English prime minister'.[67] It was broken down into identical age classes with an increasing initial interest rate depending on the class, with only minor differences to the British tontine.[68] Hamilton, did, however, develop a stipulation found in the rules of 1789 British tontine. This was the specification that when less than one per cent of nominees in any class were left alive, annuity payments would be frozen at the rate they were then at.[69] This meant that subscribers would still receive their annuity, but it would no longer increase. Hamilton planned to take this idea further than it had been taken before and to freeze annuities for each group when 20 per cent of nominees in that class remained alive.[70] Hamilton's proposal was vague on the detail, but presumably the principle saved would have reverted to the US government. As Jennings, Swanson, and Trout have argued, however, it is likely this freeze would have been 'too distant to benefit the government'.[71]

Yet, this is all academic, as Hamilton's tontine did not go ahead. But as we will see in the next chapter, the US did not need to wait long for its first tontine, with private groups initiating schemes just a few years after Hamilton's failed attempt.

Conclusion

During the eighteenth century a proliferation of public tontines emerged across Europe. What started as a relatively unsuccessful revenue-raising experiment in late-seventeenth-century France developed into a popular financial instrument used in multiple countries and regions over the next century. For cash-strapped governments, the scheme provided a way to raise revenue by securitising future obligations into current funds, while the appeal to investors came from the prospect of earning increasing annuity payments as they benefited from survivorship.

The French were proficient in tontine design, developing complex actuary structures with subdivided nominee classes to make the schemes more equitable for investors. Their tontines consistently raised the targeted subscription amounts, with some being oversubscribed. British tontines initially struggled from poor pricing and structural flaws before having some success later in the century. Outside of the major European powers, smaller nations like Ireland

and mainland European municipalities and regions also conducted their own tontine experiments to varying degrees of success.

By the mid- to late eighteenth century, however, the administration and long-term debt burden of tontines caused governments to move away from the schemes in favour of cheaper financing methods. As we will see in the next chapter, this was not the end of the tontine, as various private groups began to develop the model and initiate their own schemes.

Notes

1 D.R. Weir, 'Tontines, Public Finance, and Revolution in France and England, 1688–1789', *The Journal of Economic History*, Vol. 49, No. 1 (March, 1989), p.105.

2 While Scotland and England joined in parliamentary union in 1707, there were no government tontines operated in Scotland. As such they will be referred to as English/British tontines when talking about the schemes as a whole, and English or British when referring to specific tontines.

3 K. McKeever, 'A Short History of Tontines', *Fordham Journal of Corporate and Financial Law*, Vol. 15, Issue 42, (2009), p.494; and D.R. Weir, 'Tontines, Public Finance, and Revolution in France and England, 1688–1789', *The Journal of Economic History,* Vol. 49, No. 1 (March, 1989), p.114.

4 The first English tontine of 1693 and the French schemes of 1689 and 1696 supported the cost of the Nine Years' War (1688–1697); the French tontine of 1709 funnelled funds towards the War of the Spanish Succession (1701–1714); The War of the Polish Succession (1733–1738) was supported in part by French tontines in 1733 and 1734; French tontines of 1743, 1744 and 1745 aided the War of the Austrian succession (1740–1748); while the English tontine of 1757 and French of 1759 supported military costs associated with the Seven Years' War (1756–1763); and the English tontine of 1765 supported part of the cost of the American War of Independence (1775–1783).

5 G. Gallais-Hamonno and O. Rietsch, 'Financial Engineering in the 17th and 18th Centuries', in P. Hellwege (ed.), *The Past, Present, and Future of Tontines: A Seventeenth Century Financial Product and the Development of Life Insurance* (Berlin: Duncker & Humblot, 2018), p.66; and K. McKeever, 'A Short History of Tontines', *Fordham Journal of Corporate and Financial Law*, Vol. 15, Issue 42, (2009), pp.493–494.

6 The Grand Alliance was comprised of the Spanish who did not support Philip of Anjou, as well as England and Scotland (Great Britain after 1707), the Dutch Republic – it is worth noting that these countries were all under the same monarch, with the Dutch stadtholder, William of Orange, having ascended to the thrones of England, Scotland and Ireland, as William III & II, in 1689 – the Holy Roman Empire, Prussia, Portugal, and the Duchy of Savoy.

7 R.M. Jennings and A.P. Trout, The Tontine: From the Reign of Louis XIV to the French Revolutionary Era (Philadelphia: University of Pennsylvania, 1982), p.22; The French also sold offices. A system which allowed the buyer to purchase noble titles and receive interest on the offices they owned.

8 R.M. Jennings and A.P. Trout, *The Tontine: From the Reign of Louis XIV to the French Revolutionary Era* (Philadelphia: University of Pennsylvania, 1982), p.24.

9 R.M. Jennings and A.P. Trout, *The Tontine: From the Reign of Louis XIV to the French Revolutionary Era* (Philadelphia: University of Pennsylvania, 1982), p.24.

10 R.M. Jennings and A.P. Trout, *The Tontine: From the Reign of Louis XIV to the French Revolutionary Era* (Philadelphia: University of Pennsylvania, 1982), p.24.

11 D.R. Weir, 'Tontines, Public Finance, and Revolution in France and England, 1688–1789', *The Journal of Economic History*, Vol. 49, No. 1 (March, 1989), p.105.

12 R.M. Jennings and A.P. Trout, *The Tontine: From the Reign of Louis XIV to the French Revolutionary Era* (Philadelphia: University of Pennsylvania, 1982), p.24.

13 D.R. Weir, 'Tontines, Public Finance, and Revolution in France and England, 1688–1789', *The Journal of Economic History*, Vol. 49, No. 1 (March, 1989), p.105; and G. Gallais-Hamonno and O. Rietsch, 'Financial Engineering in the 17th and 18th Centuries', in P. Hellwege (ed.), *The Past, Present, and Future of Tontines: A Seventeenth Century Financial Product and the Development of Life Insurance* (Berlin: Duncker & Humblot, 2018), p.53.

14 D.R. Weir, 'Tontines, Public Finance, and Revolution in France and England, 1688–1789', *The Journal of Economic History*, Vol. 49, No. 1 (March, 1989), p.105.

15 D.R. Weir, 'Tontines, Public Finance, and Revolution in France and England, 1688–1789', *The Journal of Economic History*, Vol. 49, No. 1 (March, 1989), p.105.

16 D.R. Weir, 'Tontines, Public Finance, and Revolution in France and England, 1688–1789', *The Journal of Economic History*, Vol. 49, No. 1 (March, 1989), p.105 and pp.115–116.

17 D.R. Weir, 'Tontines, Public Finance, and Revolution in France and England, 1688–1789', *The Journal of Economic History*, Vol. 49, No. 1 (March, 1989), p.105, and fn47, p.117; and Y. Li and C. Rothschild, 'Adverse Selection and Redistribution in the Irish Tontines of 1773, 1775, and 1777', *Journal of Risk & Insurance, The American Risk and Insurance Association*, Vol. 87, No. 3 (2020), p.5.

18 D.R. Weir, 'Tontines, Public Finance, and Revolution in France and England, 1688–1789', *The Journal of Economic History*, Vol. 49, No. 1 (March, 1989), p.105.

19 *A List of the Nominees Appointed by the Contributors to the Tontine of the Year 1789: in Pursuance of an Act of Parliament, Made and Passed in Twenty-Ninth Year of the Reign of Our Most Gracious Sovereign King George the Third* (London: n.p., 1792), p.1; £4. 3*s*. was the starting annuity for the youngest group of nominees, and £5. 12*s*. for the oldest.

20 D.R. Weir, 'Tontines, Public Finance, and Revolution in France and England, 1688–1789', *The Journal of Economic History*, Vol. 49, No. 1 (March, 1989), p.124; and R.M. Jennings, D.F. Swanson and A.P. Trout, 'Alexander Hamilton's Tontine Proposal', *The William and Mary Quarterly*, Vol. 45, No. 1 (January, 1988), p.108.

21 M. Milevsky, *King William's Tontine: Why the Retirement Annuity of the Future Should Resemble Its Past* (Cambridge: Cambridge University Press, 2015), p.97.

22 M. Milevsky, *King William's Tontine: Why the Retirement Annuity of the Future Should Resemble Its Past* (Cambridge: Cambridge University Press, 2015), p.97; the average conversion rate between the English pound and the French livre throughout the eighteenth century was 24 to 1.

23 Gallais-Hamonno and Rietsch have calculated the modern value of £100 to be £17,100, however, as discussed in 'A Note on Money and Inflation', giving even an aproximation of the modern value is difficult See G. Gallais-Hamonno and O. Rietsch, 'Financial Engineering in the 17th and 18th Centuries', in P. Hellwege (ed.), *The Past, Present, and Future of Tontines: A Seventeenth Century Financial Product and the Development of Life Insurance* (Berlin: Duncker & Humblot, 2018), p.55.

24 G. Gallais-Hamonno and O. Rietsch, 'Financial Engineering in the 17th and 18th Centuries', in P. Hellwege (ed.), *The Past, Present, and Future of Tontines: A Seventeenth Century Financial Product and the Development of Life Insurance* (Berlin: Duncker & Humblot, 2018), pp.72–73.

25 M. Milevsky, *King William's Tontine: Why the Retirement Annuity of the Future Should Resemble Its Past* (Cambridge: Cambridge University Press, 2015), p.85; G. Clark, 'Debt, Deficits, and Crowding Out: England, 1727—1840', *European Review of Economic History*, Vol. 5, No. 3 (December, 2001), p.403; A.M. Carlos, 'British Corporate Finance, 1500–860', in G. Caprio (ed.), *Handbook of Key Global Financial Markets, Institutions, and Infrastructure* (London: Elsevier, 2013), p.45.

and R.M. Jennings, D.F. Swanson and A.P. Trout, 'Alexander Hamilton's Tontine Proposal', *The William and Mary Quarterly*, Vol. 45, No. 1 (January, 1988), p.109; There were later French public tontines of a sort, with the French revolutionary government of 1790 nationalising a private tontine which had been organised five years earlier by the duke of Orleans, and a private scheme initiated by mathematician François LaFarge, which was mired in fraud and embezzlement scandals, also being eventually nationalised. D.R. Weir, 'Tontines, Public Finance, and Revolution in France and England, 1688–1789', *The Journal of Economic History*, Vol. 49, No. 1 (March, 1989), p.96, fn.5; and P. Bourdin, translated from the French by J. Johnson, 'Truncated Democracy, Transparent Convention. The Two-thirds in the Light of the Deputies' Individual Declarations of Marital Status and Financial Assets', *Annales historiques de la Révolution française*, Vol. 381, No. 3 (2015), p.169.

26 G. Clark, 'Debt, Deficits, and Crowding Out: England, 1727—1840', *European Review of Economic History*, Vol. 5, No. 3 (December, 2001), p.403; and A.M. Carlos, 'British Corporate Finance, 1500–1860', in G. Caprio (ed.), *Handbook of Key Global Financial Markets, Institutions, and Infrastructure* London: Elsevier, 2013 p.45.

27 At this time the Irish £ traded almost at parity with £ sterling; see Y. Li and C. Rothschild, 'Adverse Selection and Redistribution in the Irish Tontines of 1773, 1775, and 1777', *Journal of Risk & Insurance, The American Risk and Insurance Association*, Vol. 87, No. 3 (2020), pp.719–750, fn1. p.723.

28 *The Statutes at Large, Passed in the Parliaments Held in Ireland: From the Third Year of Edward the Second, A.D. 1310, to the Seventh Year of George the Third, A.D. 1767, inclusive*, Volume 10 of 13 (Dublin: n.p., 1786), pp.357–366; and W. A. Thomas, *The Stock Exchanges of Ireland* (Liverpool: Francis Cairns, 1986), pp.20–21.

29 This was scrapped for subsequent Irish tontines.

30 *Freemans Journal 1763–1924*, Saturday, January 22, 1774, p.3; and *Finns Leinster Journal 1771–1828*, Wednesday, January 12, 1774, p.4.

31 Interest in the final tontine of 1777 was also slow, with the scheme only raising IR£47,000 at the initial offer of six per cent interest. After organisers made the decision to increase this to seven and a half per cent the scheme was eventually full subscribed by 1781; W.A. Thomas, *The Stock Exchanges of Ireland* (Liverpool: Francis Cairns, 1986), p.21; K. McKeever, 'A Short History of Tontines', *Fordham Journal of Corporate and Financial Law* (2009), p.494.

32 M. Milevsky, *King William's Tontine: Why the Retirement Annuity of the Future Should Resemble Its Past* (Cambridge: Cambridge University Press, 2015), p.67, p.216, and Appendix 1, pp.201–225; also included were Scottish and Welsh nominees, as well as Dutch, Italians, Spanish, and, surprisingly given what the money was being raised for, French.

33 Information on French tontines can be found in the *Belfast Newsletter*, April 30, 1762, p.2; Friday, September 01, 1769, p.2; English tontine; *Freemans Journal*, Saturday, March 16, 1765, p.2; Austrian tontine; *Freemans Journal*, Tuesday, July 16, 1765, p.2; and a Scottish tontine: *Finns Leinster Journal*, Wednesday, August 19, 1772, p.2.

34 *Belfast Newsletter*, Friday, April 30, 1762, p.2; Tuesday, May 13, 1766, p.1; Friday, September 01, 1769, p.2.

35 *Freemans Journal*, Saturday, April 06, 1765, p.2; Saturday, April 13, 1765, p.2.

36 *Freemans Journal 1763–1924*, Tuesday, November 23, 1773, p.3.

37 *Freemans Journal 1763–1924*, Tuesday, November 23, 1773, p.3; Mayne's suggestion was dismissed by various members of the House as being a method which would fail to add any liquidity to the Irish economy, as Exchequer Bills were only transferable between government and man, not between man and man. Mayne was also reminded by Tisdale, that the Irish situation differed from the English, where the powerful Bank of England could exchange cash for the Exchequer Bills, Ireland had no such bank.

38 *Freemans Journal 1763–1924,* Tuesday, November 23, 1773, p.3.
39 It is worth noting that the Dublin Corporation tried similar tontine schemes in 1775 and 1815, quite separate from the three government tontines. These were to clear debts incurred by the city. It is unclear if they went ahead.
40 A.G. Finlaison, *Report on the Mortality of Government Life Annuitants* (London, n.p., 1860), pp.79–82.
41 A.G. Finlaison, *Report on the Mortality of Government Life Annuitants* (London, n.p., 1860), pp.79–82.
42 R.M. Jennings and A.P. Trout, 'The Irish Tontine (1777) and Fifty Genevans: An Essay on Comparative Morality', *Journal of European Economic History*, Vol. 12, Issue 3, (1983), p.613.
43 R.M. Jennings and A.P. Trout, 'The Irish Tontine (1777) and Fifty Genevans: An Essay on Comparative Morality', *Journal of European Economic History*, Vol. 12, Issue 3, (1983), p.613; Irish legislation was passed in 1773 to put investors on the British mainland on an equal footing with Irish investors and to make it easier for annuities to be paid. *The Statutes at Large, Passed in the Parliaments Held in Ireland: From the Third Year of Edward the Second, A.D. 1310, to the Seventh Year of George the Third, A.D. 1767, inclusive*, Volume 10 of 13 (Dublin: n.p., 1786), pp.379–381.
44 R.M. Jennings and A.P. Trout, 'The Irish Tontine (1777) and Fifty Genevans: An Essay on Comparative Morality', *Journal of European Economic History*, Vol. 12, Issue 3, (1983), p.613; Genevan investors had been involved in the 1775 tontine, but to a far lesser extent; see C.G. Rothschild, 'Adverse Selection in Public Finance: Life-contingent Contracts in Early Modern Europe', working paper (2003), p.12; available at http://stuff.mit.edu/afs/athena/course/14/14.731/papers/adverse.pdf
45 C.G. Rothschild, 'Adverse Selection in Public Finance: Life-contingent Contracts in Early Modern Europe', working paper (2003), p.7.
46 R.M. Jennings and A.P. Trout, 'The Irish Tontine (1777) and Fifty Genevans: An Essay on Comparative Morality', *Journal of European Economic History*, Vol. 12, Issue 3, (1983), pp.613–615.
47 C.G. Rothschild, 'Adverse Selection in Public Finance: Life-contingent Contracts in Early Modern Europe', working paper (2003), p.1.
48 R.M. Jennings and A.P. Trout, 'The Irish Tontine (1777) and Fifty Genevans: An Essay on Comparative Morality', *Journal of European Economic History*, Vol. 12, Issue 3, (1983), p.613.
49 M. Fortunati, 'Tontines in Italy', in P. Hellwege (ed.), *The Past, Present, and Future of Tontines: A Seventeenth Century Financial Product and the Development of Life Insurance* (Berlin: Duncker & Humblot, 2018), p.214.
50 P. Hellwege, *A History of Tontines in Germany: From a Multi-purpose Financial Product to a Single-purpose Pension Product* (Berlin: Duncker & Humblot, 2018), p.51.
51 It is worth noting that the Dublin Corporation tried similar schemes, quite separate from the three government tontines, in 1775 and 1815. These were to clear debts incurred by the city. It is unclear if they went ahead.
52 *Finns Leinster Journal 1771–1828*, August 19,1772, p.1.
53 'Heads of the Proposed Great Edinburgh Tontine', *Caledonian Mercury*, May 5, 1836, p.3.
54 P. Hellwege, *A History of Tontines in Germany: From a Multi-purpose Financial Product to a Single-purpose Pension Product* (Berlin: Duncker & Humblot, 2018), p.50.
55 P. Hellwege, *A History of Tontines in Germany: From a Multi-purpose Financial Product to a Single-purpose Pension Product* (Berlin: Duncker & Humblot, 2018), p.80.

56 M. Fortunati, 'Tontines in Italy', in P. Hellwege (ed.), *The Past, Present, and Future of Tontines: A Seventeenth Century Financial Product and the Development of Life Insurance* (Berlin: Duncker & Humblot, 2018), pp.212–213.

57 M. Fortunati, 'Tontines in Italy', in P. Hellwege (ed.), *The Past, Present, and Future of Tontines: A Seventeenth Century Financial Product and the Development of Life Insurance* (Berlin: Duncker & Humblot, 2018), p.215.

58 M. Fortunati, 'Tontines in Italy', in P. Hellwege (ed.), *The Past, Present, and Future of Tontines: A Seventeenth Century Financial Product and the Development of Life Insurance* (Berlin: Duncker & Humblot, 2018), p.216.

59 For an overview on Scandinavian Tontines see M. Sunnqvist, 'Tontines in Scandinavia', in P. Hellwege (ed.), *The Past, Present, and Future of Tontines: A Seventeenth Century Financial Product and the Development of Life Insurance* (Berlin: Duncker & Humblot, 2018), pp.153–166.

60 M. Sunnqvist, 'Tontines in Scandinavia', in P. Hellwege (ed.), *The Past, Present, and Future of Tontines: A Seventeenth Century Financial Product and the Development of Life Insurance* (Berlin: Duncker & Humblot, 2018), p.161.

61 M. Sunnqvist, 'Tontines in Scandinavia', in P. Hellwege (ed.), *The Past, Present, and Future of Tontines: A Seventeenth Century Financial Product and the Development of Life Insurance* (Berlin: Duncker & Humblot, 2018), pp.161–162.

62 R.M. Jennings, D.F. Swanson and A.P. Trout, 'Alexander Hamilton's Tontine Proposal', *The William and Mary Quarterly*, Vol. 45, No. 1 (January, 1988), p.107; D.F. Swanson and A.P Trout, 'Alexander Hamilton's Hidden Sinking Fund', *The William and Mary Quarterly*, Vol. 49, No. 1 (January, 1992), pp.108–116.

63 R.M. Jennings, D.F. Swanson and A.P. Trout, 'Alexander Hamilton's Tontine Proposal', *The William and Mary Quarterly*, Vol. 45, No. 1 (January, 1988), p.110; D.F. Swanson and A.P. Trout, 'Alexander Hamilton, "the Celebrated Mr. Neckar," and Public Credit', *The William and Mary Quarterly*, Vol. 47, No. 3 (July, 1990), p.423;andhttps://fiscaldata.treasury.gov/americas-finance-guide/national-debt/#the-debt-ceiling.

64 R.M. Jennings, D.F. Swanson and A.P. Trout, 'Alexander Hamilton's Tontine Proposal', *The William and Mary Quarterly*, Vol. 45, No. 1 (January, 1988), p.110; and K. McKeever, 'The Evolution of the Tontine in North America', in P. Hellwege (ed.), *The Past, Present, and Future of Tontines: A Seventeenth Century Financial Product and the Development of Life Insurance* (Berlin: Duncker & Humblot, 2018), p.240.

65 J. Pons Pons, 'Comparative Analysis from the Perspective of Economic History', in P. Hellwege (ed.), *The Past, Present, and Future of Tontines: A Seventeenth Century Financial Product and the Development of Life Insurance* (Berlin: Duncker & Humblot, 2018), p.369.

66 J. Pons Pons, 'Comparative Analysis from the Perspective of Economic History', in P. Hellwege (ed.), *The Past, Present, and Future of Tontines: A Seventeenth Century Financial Product and the Development of Life Insurance* (Berlin: Duncker & Humblot, 2018).

67 D.F. Swanson and A.P. Trout, 'Alexander Hamilton, "the Celebrated Mr. Neckar," and Public Credit', *The William and Mary Quarterly*, Vol. 47, No. 3 (July, 1990), p.427.

68 R.M. Jennings, D.F. Swanson and A.P. Trout, 'Alexander Hamilton's Tontine Proposal', *The William and Mary Quarterly*, Vol. 45, No. 1 (January, 1988), p.112.

69 R.M. Jennings, D.F. Swanson and A.P. Trout, 'Alexander Hamilton's Tontine Proposal', *The William and Mary Quarterly*, Vol. 45, No. 1 (January, 1988), p.111.

70 K. McKeever, 'A Short History of Tontines', *Fordham Journal of Corporate and Financial Law* (2009), p.495.

71 R.M. Jennings, D.F. Swanson and A.P. Trout, 'Alexander Hamilton's Tontine Proposal', *The William and Mary Quarterly*, Vol. 45, No. 1 (January, 1988), p.115.

Bibliography

Primary Sources

A List of the Nominees Appointed by the Contributors to the Tontine of the Year 1789: in Pursuance of an Act of Parliament, Made and Passed in Twenty-Ninth Year of the Reign of Our Most Gracious Sovereign King George the Third (London: n.p., 1792)

Butler, J.G. (ed.), *The Statutes at Large, Passed in the Parliaments Held in Ireland: From the Third Year of Edward the Second, A.D. 1310, to the Seventh Year of George the Third, A.D. 1767, Inclusive*, Volume 10 of 13 (Dublin: n.p., 1786).

Finlaison, A.G., *Report on the Mortality of Government Life Annuitants* (London, n.p., 1860).

Finns Leinster Journal, August 19, 1772.

'Heads of the Proposed Great Edinburgh Tontine', *Caledonian Mercury*, Thursday, May 5, 1836.

Books

Hellwege, P., *A History of Tontines in Germany: From a Multi-purpose Financial Product to a Single-purpose Pension Product* (Berlin: Duncker & Humblot, 2018).

Jennings, R.M. and Trout, A.P., *The Tontine: From the Reign of Louis XIV to the French Revolutionary Era* (Philadelphia: University of Pennsylvania, 1982).

Milevsky, M., *King William's Tontine: Why the Retirement Annuity of the Future Should Resemble Its Past* (Cambridge: Cambridge University Press, 2015).

Thomas, W.A., *The Stock Exchanges of Ireland* (Liverpool: Francis Cairns, 1986).

Edited Collections and Journal Articles

Bourdin P., translated from the French by Johnson, J., 'Truncated Democracy, Transparent Convention. The Two-thirds in the Light of the Deputies' Individual Declarations of Marital Status and Financial Assets', in *Annales historiques de la Révolution française,* Vol. 381, No. 3 (2015), pp.155–187.

Carlos, A.M., 'British Corporate Finance, 1500–1860', in Caprio, G. (ed.), *Handbook of Key Global Financial Markets, Institutions, and Infrastructure* (London: Elsevier, 2013), pp. 39–46

Clark, G., 'Debt, Deficits, and Crowding Out: England, 1727---1840', *European Review of Economic History*, Vol. 5, No. 3 (2001), pp.403–436.

Gallais-Hamonno, G. and Rietsch, O., 'Financial Engineering in the 17th and 18th Centuries', in Hellwege, P. (ed.), *The Past, Present, and Future of Tontines: A Seventeenth Century Financial Product and the Development of Life Insurance* (Berlin: Duncker & Humblot, 2018), pp.49–78.

Jennings, R.M. and Trout, A.P., 'The Irish Tontine (1777) and Fifty Genevans: An Essay on Comparative Morality', *Journal of European Economic History*, Vol. 12, Issue 3, (1983), pp.611–618.

Jennings, R.M., Swanson, D.F. and Trout, A.P., 'Alexander Hamilton's Tontine Proposal', *The William and Mary Quarterly*, Vol. 45, No. 1 (1988), pp.107–115.

Li, Y. and Rothschild, C., 'Adverse Selection and Redistribution in the Irish Tontines of 1773, 1775, and 1777', *Journal of Risk & Insurance, The American Risk and Insurance Association*, Vol. 87 (2020), pp.719–750.

McKeever, K., 'A Short History of Tontines', *Fordham Journal of Corporate and Financial Law*, Vol. 15, Issue 42, (2009), pp.491–521.

McKeever, K., 'The Evolution of the Tontine in North America', in Hellwege, P. (ed.), *The Past, Present, and Future of Tontines: A Seventeenth Century Financial Product and the Development of Life Insurance* (Berlin: Duncker & Humblot, 2018), pp.193–202.

Pons Pons, J., 'Comparative Analysis from the Perspective of Economic History', in Hellwege, P. (ed.), *The Past, Present, and Future of Tontines: A Seventeenth Century Financial Product and the Development of Life Insurance* (Berlin: Duncker & Humblot, 2018), pp.367–382.

Rothschild, C.G., 'Adverse Selection in Public Finance: Life-contingent Contracts in Early Modern Europe', working paper, MIT (2003).

Sunnqvist, M., 'Tontines in Scandinavia', in Hellwege, P. (ed.), *The Past, Present, and Future of Tontines: A Seventeenth Century Financial Product and the Development of Life Insurance* (Berlin: Duncker & Humblot, 2018), pp.153–166.

Swanson, D.F. and Trout, A.P., 'Alexander Hamilton, "the Celebrated Mr. Neckar," and Public Credit', *The William and Mary Quarterly*, Vol. 47, No. 3 (July, 1990), pp.422–430.

Swanson, D.F. and Trout, A.P., 'Alexander Hamilton's Hidden Sinking Fund', in *The William and Mary Quarterly*, Vol. 49, No. 1 (January, 1992), pp.108–116.

Weir, D.R., 'Tontines, Public Finance, and Revolution in France and England, 1688–1789', *The Journal of Economic History*, Vol. 49, No. 1 (1989), pp.95–126.

4 Private Tontines in Great Britain and Ireland, Europe, and North America

1750–1900

The second half of the eighteenth century marked a turning point for the tontine as a large-scale public revenue-raising tool. Governments had become increasingly aware that borrowing from lenders at lower interest rates or selling bonds with lower repayment rates, were far more fiscally responsible ways to raise funds. As public schemes were being wound down, a new offering of smaller tontines operated by private, usually local, groups began to emerge. These were sometimes short term investment schemes of five to seven years, where the tontine fund was invested in a stock of some sort and dividends paid from the money generated. At other times they were used to fund the cost of civic improvement projects and private buildings.

This chapter will cover the development of private tontines throughout the four nations that made up Great Britain and Ireland, as well as the United States and areas within mainland Europe. It will demonstrate that the tontine supported the cost of buildings that enlarged the public sphere, bringing people together to share news and debate. It financed the construction of theatres and libraries, providing spaces for education and the sharing of culture. Church buildings were established with tontine funding, as were private homes, public meeting rooms, and even prisons. And infrastructure projects, including streets, bridges, and canals were financed via the scheme. As will become clear, the tontine really was everywhere.

Also addressed in this chapter are the mutual aid tontines which became particularly popular in Ireland during the nineteenth century. These were most often set up as sickness and burial clubs, paying out to subscribers when required, with any residual funds being divided among participants at Christmas each year. The mutual aid tontine was significant for being the first Irish tontine model that was directed at the country's working classes and poor.

Private Tontines in Great Britain and Ireland

By the last quarter of the eighteenth century, the establishment of private tontines in Britain and Ireland was being carried out with startling regularity. In mainland Britain these were largely of the two forms already outlined; one

DOI: 10.4324/9781003491002-4

to raise an investment fund and the other to finance civic improvement and building projects.

When established as an investment fund, a popular stock to invest in was British government consols. These were bonds which offered investors a three per cent return and provided the government with access to cheaper borrowing from the 1750s onwards; ironically the consols were also instrumental in reducing the attractiveness of tontines as a government revenue-raising tool.[1]

Tontines directed at financing building projects, meanwhile, covered a diverse range of ventures. These included assembly rooms, coffeehouses, theatres, hotels and homes, and infrastructure projects such as streets and bridges. In most cases, this form of tontine was organised by, and catered for, wealthier members of society. Subscriptions were expensive and investment was largely drawn from the professional classes, including bankers and lawyers; local elites; politicians; and the mercantile community. The involvement of these groups determined the kinds of projects funded via tontine and meant that investment was usually directed at venues which supported business, allowed for the sharing of news, and provided spaces for socialising and entertainment. Subscribers to these tontines were paid their annuities from rents, profits, or tolls, depending on the project. As with other tontines, the annuity increased with benefit of survivorship, with the bonus that subscribers often had the opportunity to 'win' ownership of the completed project, be that a coffeehouse, hotel, or any other building, if their nominee managed to be the last surviving in the scheme.

These tontines became a popular way to finance civic improvement and urban development at a time when the ability of many local councils to do this was restricted. For councils to undertake these types of projects it would mean increasing taxes (an unpopular move) or borrowing (which due to a weak banking system anywhere outside of London was restricted; particularly from the 1790s when private lending was squeezed out by government borrowing to fund the national debt).[2] The tontine therefore allowed private groups to raise money locally for projects which would benefit the local area.

England

While scholarly work on the tontine continues to develop, England has been relatively well-served by the existing literature. The use of tontines to fund civic improvements in Georgian Britain, in particular England, has been explored by David Green, providing an important addition to the historiography.[3] Likewise, a very robust piece of unpublished work on the 1775 Freemasons' Tontine in London by Diane Clements has also been a welcome addition to the literature.[4] Meanwhile, Moshe Milevsky's work on the English government tontine of 1693 has done much to illuminate our wider understanding of tontines in the country.[5] Through these works and other research, at least 216 private tontines, active and proposed, have so far been identified in England between 1750 and 1880.[6] (This does not include the mutual aid tontines in England which will later be discussed within an Irish context.)

Of the known English tontines, 55 appear to have been investment schemes of some sort, with the rest directed at building projects. The earliest active investment tontine originated in the west London town of Uxbridge in 1785 and raised £30,000.[7] A few years later, likely inspired by the contemporaneous British government tontine of 1789, a boom in private tontines commenced, with at least 33 English schemes in existence by 1792. These could be found across the country, and included Hungerford, Frome and Exeter (1789); Carlisle, Lichfield and Ipswich (1790); Bath, Rochester and Bristol (1791); and Maidstone, Trowbridge and Winchester (1792). A further eight investment tontines were established or proposed before the end of the eighteenth century, after which they continued to operate but with less frequency. Only 11 schemes can be identified between 1800 and 1825, after which interest in the tontine as an investment instrument of this sort appears to have dwindled.[8]

When it comes to project financing via tontines, the earliest example comes from Bristol in 1754. This raised £3600 to fund the cost of building assembly rooms in the city.[9] This was the first of at least 12 tontines established in Bristol during the next eight decades, as the city became a hub of tontine activity.[10] The tontine's popularity was largely matched across England, with it being unusual for an English county not to have at least one in operation.[11] The projects funded with the scheme included a Library in Birmingham (1799); three tontines to build a house of corrections in Middlesex (1790, 1793, 1795); a workhouse in Coventry (1801); hotels in Chelmsford (1801), Plymouth (1810) and Dawlish (1812); and theatres in Bath and Plymouth (both 1805); and a church in Wallsend (1804).[12]

There was a particular concentration of tontines around London, with at least 39 proposed or established there between 1674 and 1879. As stated in Chapter 2 the earliest examples from London emerged from the City of London; these were two investment tontines (1674 and 1683) which do not appear to have been set in motion.[13] Once the tontine did get off the ground in the English capital, however, it was directed at myriad projects. These included a plan to raise £816,000 for the construction of docks (1797); funds to underwrite the cost of the Regents Canal (1817) and Alexandra Palace (1870); a tontine to cover the cost of chambers which housed 500 offices for lawyers and parliamentary agents at the Palace of Westminster (1863); and a tontine opera house on the Thames embankment (1879).[14] While investment tontines had therefore decreased in popularity by the mid-1820s, project funding via tontine remained active for at least another five decades.

Many of the projects built with money raised in a tontine still exist today, but unless the word 'tontine' has been retained in their name, such as the Cleveland Tontine, a hotel in North Yorkshire, or the Tontine Buildings in

Cirencester, Gloucestershire, their origins are often obscure at best, or at worst lost. Take London's Richmond Bridge, for example, finished in 1777, it spans the Thames and is the city's oldest crossing of the river. A plan was put in place to finance the £25,000 needed for the bridge through a tontine in 1773.[15] Legislation was passed for the project in July of that year, and within five months £12,000 in subscriptions had been pledged.[16] In addition, the proprietor who held the ferry rights at the Richmond crossing offered to relinquish his privileges if the bridge commissioners provided him with £6,000, which he committed to reinvesting in the bridge.[17] Despite the funds pledged, this initial plan was abandoned due to an apparent lack of interest.[18]

A new proposal followed in April of 1774, this time for the lower amount of £20,000 to be raised through the sale of 200 shares priced at £100 each, with annuities being paid from bridge tolls.[19] By the middle of May the new scheme was fully subscribed, drawing subscriptions largely from the local area and London more widely.[20] By reducing the amount of the initial tontine, the bridge commissioners had bought themselves time to construct the bridge and start to levy tolls and pay annuities. The sum of £20,000 was not enough to fully finish the crossing, however, and in 1776 a second tontine was initiated for the sum of £5,000.[21] The bridge was then fully completed the following year. The last nominee lived until 1859, collecting an £800 annuity for the subscriber, after which the bridge became toll-free.[22] One wonders how many of those who use the bridge today are aware of how it was funded?

Scotland

Scotland, unlike England and Ireland, was never the site of a government tontine. Setting up a public tontine was in fact never formally discussed by Scottish representatives in the country's parliament at any point between the first English tontine of 1693 and 1707, the year in which the Anglo-Scots Union brought Scotland and England together under one parliament.[23] Nor did the British parliament seek to implement a tontine in Scotland after 1707. Several factors likely contributed to this outcome.

First, Scotland in the early 1690s was a 'financially confident' country.[24] Many had done well from the revolution of 1688–1689, and during the first half of the 1690s, the country witnessed something of a business boom, with 47 joint-stock companies in operation. These included new small to medium factories producing various goods, as well as the large joint-stock offerings of the Bank of Scotland – which issued a significant amount of circulating currency into the economy during the second half of the decade – and the Company of Scotland; the group behind the attempt to establish a Scottish colony on the Isthmus of Darien, in South America.[25] It therefore seems that Scottish attention was not on establishing a tontine, but on business and colonisation. Second, as some readers may know, the attempt on Darien was an abject failure. Poor planning, mismanagement, disease, colonist in-fighting, a lack of support from the crown, and the presence of the Spanish, all combined to derail Scotland's grand project. The financial fall-out was so severe, that Scottish parliamentarians were too burned by the experience to undertake any new financial risks.[26] Third, as discussed in Chapter 2, English and French tontines of the late seventeenth century had been met with limited success, pulling in a fraction of the sums they had intended and likely making the Scottish government sceptical of the scheme's usefulness.[27] Lastly, in the years which followed the Union, the new British government, showed little interest in the financial fortunes of Scotland; a situation only altered in the aftermath of the Jacobite uprising in 1715, and after a series of riots linked to food, anti-enclosure, and the Malt Tax in the first half of the 1720s.[28] A government tontine in Scotland was therefore not considered by either pre- or post-Union governments.

Despite the absence of public schemes, private tontines were embraced in Scotland during the second half of the eighteenth century. The background to this popularity was driven in part by a lack of public money. Funding local projects was a problem that plagued Scottish burghs throughout the eighteenth and nineteenth centuries.[29] Locally raised revenue such as rental income, tolls and other means, was rarely enough to undertake substantial urban development, meaning that additional funding was often sought at both a local and national level. A burgh administration could combine with a group of local investors to fund buildings such as meeting rooms and markets. Burghs could also make financial assistance applications to Scotland's Convention of Estates, a group made up of nobles, clergy, and representatives from the burghs, and by the 1790s it became increasingly normal for Scotland's burghs to petition the British parliament to pass specific legislation to fund urban improvement.[30] It was also common for local authorities to apply to the national executive for the right to place a tax on ale to raise extra income to fund local developments. As one might imagine, this method was unpopular, as was the raising of money through the enclosure of common lands, with both processes usually failing to raise any significant sums anyway. There were therefore a variety of funding options, but this did not stop a slew of local authority bankruptcies around the turn of the nineteenth century. It was against this backdrop of cash-strapped local administrations and a need for urban improvement, that the tontine emerged as an important funding instrument in Scotland.[31]

Between the 1770s and the 1850s the tontine was employed in Scotland as both an investment tool and as a method of raising funds for building projects. At least 40 active or proposed tontines have been identified during this period, although there were undoubtedly more.[32] The scheme was used across the country from Greenock and Ardrossan in the lowland west, to Cupar and Dundee in the east, and from the border's town of Peebles to Inverness in the north. Eight of the tontines operated as investment schemes of varying size. A fund in Glasgow, for example, sought to raise £20,000 in 1816, while another intended to raise the lower sum of £7,200 in the Stirlingshire town of Alva in 1841, both invested their fund in stock of some form.[33] The remaining private Scottish tontines were directed at raising capital to fund a building project of some sort. These included hotels, taverns, assembly rooms, and public baths; members-only clubs and coffeerooms; entertainment spaces such as theatres and concert halls; and private dwellings.[34]

As might be expected, there was a concentration of at least 22 tontines in Glasgow and Edinburgh combined. Of the schemes that are presently known, ten operated or were proposed in the Scottish capital between 1790 and 1826. Five of these were investment tontines, and included two unsuccessful attempts (1797 and 1807) by Thomas Hopkirk, a director at the Royal Bank of Scotland between 1807 and 1821.[35] The other five tontines were used to fund building projects, including a tontine building in Leith (1812), the Union Clubhouse (1823), about which little information can be sourced, and two hotels, one on Princes Street and one on George Street, both built in the early 1790s.[36]

In Glasgow and the surrounding area, 12 tontines existed between 1781 and 1844. Of these, two were investment tontines, while the rest were directed at the costs of private residences and public venues. The latter included tenement blocks, theatres, assembly rooms, and hotels, with perhaps the best known being the 1781 scheme to develop the Tontine Buildings in Glasgow's Trongate. The site included a coffee-room, assembly rooms, a tavern and lodgings, and drew its investment of £5350 through the sale of 107 tontine shares mainly to local merchants; only three subscribers came from outside of the Glasgow area.[37] The coffee-room was a particularly important space for Glasgow's movers and shakers, and was really a newsroom where commerce, academia, and print culture intermingled.[38] Here members could view advertisements, consult shipping lists, and access British and European newspapers, periodicals, and pamphlets.[39]

As was the case elsewhere, tontine-funded buildings in Scotland developed as important spaces for bringing people together to share news, discuss national and local matters, to conduct political meetings, and for entertainment. Advertisements and news stories carried in the Scottish press demonstrate the importance of these spaces and the type of business being carried out in them. Creditors meetings, for example, were held in tontine hotels. Sales of land, ships, coal, and wine among other commodities took place in the Glasgow Tontine Sale-Room, in tontine taverns in Edinburgh and Glasgow, and in Greenock's Tontine Hotel. Local dignitaries used the spaces for official business; such as when the Lord Provost of Glasgow entertained the Duke of Hamilton and bequeathed him with the freedom of the city in Glasgow's Tontine Tavern in 1800.[40] Or when British prime minister, John Russell, was on his way to Balmoral Castle in 1848 and stopped in and stayed at the Tontine

Hotel in Greenock.[41] And when tragedy struck with the explosion of a steamer crossing the Firth of Clyde in 1842, it was to the Tontine Hotel in Helensburgh that the bodies were taken for identification. [42] Tontine-funded spaces in Scotland were clearly important to the communities which built them.

Before we leave Scotland, there is the interesting example of the Islay Tontine Life Association. This was an 1849 scheme which raised £600,000, comprised of 12,000 shares at £50 each, to purchase the estate of Islay, consisting of the island itself and the islets which surrounded it. This group operated out of Glasgow and Edinburgh, and included directors of both the Bank of Scotland and the Royal Bank of Scotland (RBS) in its ranks.[43] The managing director of the association was Archibald Murdoch Burrell, then provost of Port Glasgow and a banker with RBS; three other RBS directors were also among the Islay Tontine Life Association's twelve directors. The group successfully purchased the estate in August 1849 for £530,000, but by early 1850 it was reported in the Scottish press that the Islay estate was to be 'again offered for public sale, the tontine scheme having proved a failure'.[44] Despite this, the Islay scheme is notable for including a particularly novel form of protection to safeguard investors.

A central risk of any tontine was that a subscriber's nominee would die prematurely and prohibit the subscriber not only from making a profit, but from recouping their initial investment. The structure of the Islay tontine sought to mitigate this risk in an innovative way by insuring the life of every nominee with a separate life insurance policy. This meant that upon the death of a nominee, the subscriber would receive back their full subscription fee.[45] While this was of course something that any tontine subscriber could do independently, it was a complicated process. Hedging your bet in this manner required the tontine subscriber to work out the probabilities of returns on the system and calculate whether the expensive price of the life insurance policy was worth the return, or if it was better to take the chance with the tontine. These were calculations which were beyond most people.[46] So, while private life insurance on tontine nominees was possible prior to the Islay Tontine Life Association scheme, it is difficult to say whether it was common. Bundling this in as part of the tontine package made things much simpler and was one of the most innovative developments of the model since Tonti's plan of 1653.

Ireland

Of any country that utilised tontines, Ireland has one of the most interesting histories. First, it was the site of three successful government tontines in the 1770s. Then, between the 1790s and 1820s, private groups organised a handful of schemes directed at building costs, investment funds, and private debts. The country was also the source of a novel form of mutual aid tontine model directed at the working classes and poor from the 1830s onwards. In addition, a very interesting temperance tontine, designed to keep members sober, also emerged in the middle decades of the nineteenth century.[47] The case of Ireland therefore illustrates the diverse ways in which the tontine principle could be applied.

The private schemes directed at investment and building costs, as were popular in England and Scotland, were less so in Ireland. While there were more than 200 private tontines in England and at least 40 in Scotland between around 1750 and 1880, in Ireland just 17 have been identified. Five of these were investment tontines; three in Dublin (1776, 1791, 1815), one in Belfast (1791), and one which was a joint venture between bankers in Dublin and Cork (1792). Two were established by landholders to pay off private debts. While the other 10 private tontines were directed at civic improvement and urban development projects. The majority of these went towards the costs of private homes and included five schemes in and around Limerick; the George Street Tontine (1806), the Richmond Place West Tontine (1807), the Richmond Place East Tontine (between 1805 and 1809), Castleconnell Tontine (1812), and the Pery Square Tontine (1834); as well as one in Ennis in 1836.[48] There was also a tontine directed at infrastructure costs, with £200,000 being raised to clear the debts of Dublin's Grand Canal Company and carry out further works in 1791, and a failed attempt to finance a new thoroughfare in Dublin, to be named Great Wellesley Street, in 1838.[49] Meanwhile, the types of tontine-funded spaces which were popular in Scotland and England, were less so in Ireland, with only two examples, a coffeehouse in Cork and assembly rooms in Armagh, existing. Both do, however, provide interesting insights into the importance of these spaces in their communities.

Established in 1793, the Cork Coffeehouse was likely the earliest Irish private tontine directed at building work. This raised £3,500 via 140 shares priced at £25 each, and, in addition to the coffeehouse, provided space for shops, apartments, and three houses.[50] The shares were purchased by 116 individual subscribers, 61 of which were merchants. The rest were drawn from professions such as bankers and lawyers, and from local elites; even the city's mayor invested.[51] Situated on Castle Street, close to the city's exchange, numerous banks and booksellers, and various taverns, Cork's Tontine Coffeehouse became a prime meeting spot. Not only was it where the most up to date news from London and Europe could be read, it also acted as the venue for political meetings and military courts, and it was where local and national petitions, such as the 1812 petition for Protestants in favour of Catholic emancipation, could be signed.[52] The coffeehouse was therefore an important local venue for Corkonians.

A year after the Cork tontine had commenced in 1793, a scheme to fund the building of assembly rooms in Armagh, in the north of the country, was established. The result was a members-only premises charging 5s. 5d. per quarter, which hosted dances, business functions, and social gatherings.[53] The fee meant that the building was not open to everyone, but this changed in the 1820s, when, in the face of declining fortunes, new trustees focused on making the rooms accessible to all and took the decision to scrap the membership costs. By 1840 the building had expanded to include 'a suite of apartments

…, a public news-room, and a savings bank', and had become an important location for community meetings, including local societies, temperance groups, and religious groups.[54] The rooms also acted as a venue for visiting shows and public talks, ranging from magicians and ventriloquists to poet and playwright, Oscar Wilde.[55] While tontine-funded spaces were therefore less prevalent in Ireland, than in Scotland and England, they were no less important to the communities where they did exist.

The last two examples of private Irish tontines were directed at covering private debts. The first was established in 1789 by Edmund Boyle, the seventh earl of Cork and the seventh earl of Orrery. The scheme, which appears to have been well subscribed, paid the annuities due from the rents and profits of Boyle's Irish estates.[56] As the majority of subscribers were English, and Boyle was born and died in Frome, Somerset, it appears to have been yet another example of an absentee landlord withdrawing wealth from Ireland. The second was run in 1792 by Charles O'Hara Jr, a representative in the Irish and British parliaments. The plan, which was intended to raise £33,000, was the latest of several attempts by O'Hara, and his father before him, to improve the family's financial situation.[57] Well known as improving landlords the O'Hara's had previously attempted to introduce mining and weaving into their estates. A move which proved unsuccessful and left the family in debt.[58] The tontine, which was secured on the family's Coolany estate and 45 other pieces of land held in County Sligo, therefore provided some much-needed financial support for O'Hara.[59] As with all tontines, however, it was not a quick fix, and tied the family to paying annuities to subscribers until the 1880s.[60]

Aside from the private tontines already discussed, from the 1830s there also existed a mutual aid model of the scheme directed at the Irish working classes and poor. These combined an insurance instrument with a tontine, and offered subscribers a sickness and burial benefit, or in some cases access to a benevolent fund, in exchange for a weekly subscription. The tontine function of the scheme was derived from the practice of dividing any remaining funds among subscribers at Christmas, with only subscribers who had not claimed a benefit during the year being eligible for a share. After the payout the scheme was then wound up, with a small amount kept back to cover the costs of restarting the tontine, usually equivalent to one subscriber's benefit, and the process was renewed in the next year.

Mutual aid tontines existed in Ireland among a network of other small local schemes offering funeral and sickness benefits which were administered by a mixture of friendly and benevolent societies, trade groups, and religious groups. These were hugely popular. If we take the year 1869 as an example, 224 mutual aid schemes existed in Ireland, with 42,703 members and a geographical spread which covered the whole country.[61] 34 of these schemes were registered as tontines, with a total membership of 1,704 (we can also assume that there were many groups that chose not to register).[62] Mutual aid tontines therefore represented around 15 per cent of the total market in these types of schemes in Ireland at this time. Many were religiously affiliated, with 63 of the 92 registered between 1833 and 1877 falling into this category. Others were linked to trades, such as the Ropemakers Tontine or the Dublin Mechanical Tontine. While others, such as the Celtic Tontine and the Harp and Shamrock Tontine, wore their Irishness on their sleeves.[63]

The mutual aid tontine also existed in England but was very much an Irish financial instrument which should be considered within an Irish context. These were largely located in and around Liverpool, a city with a population of 375,955 by 1851, of which 83,813 had been born in Ireland, equating to 22.3 per cent.[64] As I have argued elsewhere, the existence of mutual aid tontines in this area was as a direct result of Irish immigrant communities drawing on their cultural knowledge and transplanting supporting structures into England.[65] If we take the 1862 *Report of the Registrar of Friendly Societies in England* as an example, there were 57 mutual aid tontines recorded. All but one was located in the Merseyside area of Lancashire, predominantly in and around the city of Liverpool.[66] The report for the following year matches this pattern, with 57 out of 58 tontines located in Merseyside; the one tontine which was not, was based in London but was named the Mersey Docks Benefit Tontine.[67] This correlation continued in future reports; with the 1866 report citing 56 tontines all located in the Liverpool area, while the 1874 report provided details on 36 similarly located tontines.[68] The appearance of the mutual aid tontine in England therefore correlates closely with the existence of migrant Irish communities.

The last configuration of Irish tontine to be considered is the rather unusual temperance tontine. These attempted to financially incentivise sobriety, with payment of tontine annuities linked to subscribers' abstinence. At least seven operated in Dublin between 1839 and 1862, with one also in Portlaw, County Waterford from 1838, and another in County Wexford.[69] These were organised in a similar manner to the mutual aid tontine, with weekly subscriptions and a yearly payout, but without an inbuilt insurance instrument. The premise was straightforward: subscribers were required to make a regular payment into the fund, and, if come the end of the year they had maintained their sobriety, they received a share in the accumulated total. How much they got was dependent on several variables; how many other subscribers had enrolled in the scheme; how many had managed to abstain from alcohol; and of those who had failed, how much they had paid into the fund by the time they fell off the wagon.

These schemes emerged at a time when Friendly Societies were increasingly defining themselves by their abstinence stance after 1839 and can be viewed within the wider Irish Temperance movement which was gaining ground in the middle decades of the nineteenth century.[70] That said, these were not an exclusively Irish phenomenon, with a 'Tee Total Tontine' also established in the Ayrshire village of Dalry in 1838.[71] No doubt more existed.

Wales

Of the four countries which made up the United Kingdom of Great Britain and Ireland, Wales appears to have been the site of the least tontine activity. Like

Scotland, there was never a Welsh public tontine, nor did the country embrace investment tontines. Tontines directed at building projects were proposed but were limited, with only five being identified between 1791 and 1832. These included plans for an inn in Merthyr-Tydfil (1805), and for tontine hotels in the north-eastern seaside resort of Rhyl (1829) and in Caswell Bay in the south-east (1832); although it is unclear if any scheme was realised.[72] Where things are more certain, is with two very interesting examples of Welsh tontines, one to fund the costs of building a theatre, and the other a street of houses, both in Swansea.

The Swansea Tontine Association, formed in 1791, was most likely the earliest Welsh tontine society. Made up of 100 subscribers, the fund was used to build five houses on Tontine Street. Annuities were paid from the rent collected, and when the last 10 subscribers remained, they had the choice either to sell the properties and split the proceeds, or to carry on until five were left, at which point they would each take ownership of one of the houses.[73] The scheme was an early example of tontine funding being used to build private homes, with more emerging in other regions of the UK and Ireland during the first half of the 1800s. These were generally grand affairs, take the example of the opulent Georgian buildings in Pery Square Limerick (1834), or the similarly grand facades of Glasgow's Regent Street (1836) which were funded via tontine. By comparison Swansea's Tontine Street was a far more ordinary block of small, terraced houses, which provided homes for factory and dock workers.[74] Over the next century the street does not appear to have fared well and when referenced in the local press, which was often, it was usually in less than glowing terms, with complaints of overcrowding, drunkenness, fighting, and thefts being common.[75]

The Swansea Theatre Tontine by contrast appears to have been a much more refined affair. Established in 1805, in a push from the city's 'leisured classes', it was who hoped that the resultant venue and its accompanying assembly rooms would attract a fashionable clientele.[76] Supported by the great and the good of Swansea, the scheme collected £3,000 through the sale of 300 £10 shares.[77] While it was initially a success, with the theatre fulfilling its purpose of being a stylish venue throughout much of the nineteenth century, the closing decades of the century proved difficult. There were financial challenges in maintaining the ageing theatre, with the site's owners falling behind in the provision of safety precautions for visitors. Less money was also coming in through ticket sales, as music halls emerged in competition and poached many of its customers.

There were also real difficulties in managing the tontine, as it became harder and harder to verify whether a nominee was alive or dead. In 1878, for example, when 128 subscribers were still active in the tontine, 99 of them could not be located. This required the society to undertake the administratively burdensome and financially costly task of placing advertisements in the local and national press to trace those with an interest in the theatre.[78] This demonstrates just how difficult it could be to administer a tontine, and was, as David Green has pointed out, not an isolated incident, with an increase in 'personal mobility' at this time making 'the issue of locating tontine subscribers and nominees' more difficult.[79]

Tensions between theatre management and the tontine society, and within the society itself, also became more common, with the last years of the Swansea Theatre Tontine marked by legal wrangles over outstanding repair costs, and the desire of some to sell the venue.[80] The venture was wound up in 1891, with just over £835 being shared between four remaining shareholders.[81]

In addition to providing project funding, Welsh press reports indicate that there was also some mutual aid tontine activity in the country. These appear to have emerged much later than they did in either Ireland or England, with the earliest example being set up in the small village of Kerry, in the county of Powys in 1870.[82] Three further schemes followed in the next decade, one in the town of Dolgellau (1873) and two in Wrexham (1876 and 1880).[83] From the early 1890s this type of tontine activity appears to have increased significantly. With a newspaper report from late December 1892, detailing that the Welsh tontine societies, which had 'sprang up of late with such remarkable rapidity', then numbered 17.[84]

It appears that Welsh mutual aid tontines operated in an analogous manner to those offered in Ireland and England, providing a sickness and funeral benefit when required, and with a Christmas division of surplus funds. While there will undoubtedly be other Welsh mutual aid tontines, the indicators are that these were popular during the 1890s and into the next century, but appear to have been limited, certainly in comparison to the numbers of these schemes operating in Ireland and England.[85] Presently it is not possible to say if they were directly influenced by Irish mutual aid tontines or by English schemes.

Private Tontines in Mainland Europe

As covered in Chapter 2, private investment tontines were very popular in the Dutch Republic in the closing decades of the seventeenth century. Almost 200 of these were set up between 1670 and 1700, after which, in the face of a fraud scandal, numbers decreased, but by no means ceased altogether, with at least 100 private investment tontines established during the next century.[86] The eighteenth century also saw the promotion of a limited number of tontines to fund building projects in the Dutch Republic.

This included an attempt in 1763 to fund the building of a sea harbour in the municipality of Harderwijk. This was not quite a private or a public tontine, but a coming together of both, and was set afoot by group of contractors entering into an agreement with the city's lawmakers. The harbour was to be funded via a standard tontine made up of subscriptions and paying investors an annuity which increased with benefit of survivorship. In exchange for building the harbour, the contractors were to hold exclusive rights to its use for 40 years, after which the city would take ownership, pay the contractors 200,000 guilders, and become responsible for any tontine annuities that were still active.[87] This was a grand plan which illustrates how the tontine could be used, but was not one which went ultimately ahead.

As the popularity of private tontines then continued to grow in other regions of Europe during the first half of the nineteenth century, it sharply declined in the Netherlands. This was particularly pronounced after the end of the Dutch Republic in 1795, with only six investment tontines (two private and four by religious groups) identified between that year and 1815.[88]

In the German states and German-speaking territories, meanwhile, there is often a lack of clarity around tontines. Phillip Hellwege, when preparing a history of German tontines, initially compiled a list comprised of 57 schemes across the seventeenth and eighteenth centuries. This was collated from references to the tontine in modern literature and in the contemporary literature of the period, and in various German archives. On closer inspection, however, Hellwege found that many of these 'tontines' were in fact lotteries or life annuities with no tontine function present. After the list had been narrowed to only those which operated with a tontine principle, 18 schemes remained, some of which did not get past the planning stage.[89] Of those that did get off the ground, many were operated by states or municipalities as discussed in the previous chapter. Of the limited tontines that we might class as private, there is not one example of a scheme being used to fund the building of a space of some sort, and instead these appear to have been exclusively investment instruments. As Hellwege has stated, tontines in Germany were not 'everyday transactions'.[90]

In mainland Europe therefore it appears that private tontines existed primary as investment funds and as insurance instruments, and rarely as a means of financing building projects. This was the case in the Netherlands, the German territories, the Italian states, Spain, the Scandinavian countries, France, and Hungary.[91]

Private Tontines in North America

Examples of private tontines in North America are limited. While some operated in Canada and the Caribbean, the majority of this type of activity was to be found in the United States.[92] This included two hotels; one in New Haven, Connecticut (1824) and another in Brunswick, Maine (1828); coffeehouses in Albany, New York (sometime during the 1790s) and in New York City (1793); and a block of private apartments in Boston, Massachusetts (1793).[93] Despite their apparently small number, the country was the site of two very interesting tontines, one for its legacy and the other for the debate which it ignited.

Established in 1793, the Tontine Association of New York raised $40,600 to build the Tontine Coffee House.[94] The plan was set in motion by a group of stockbrokers and merchants, who had one year earlier signed an agreement to broker deals only with one another, and to charge a set 0.25 per cent commission on their trades. Known as the Buttonwood Agreement, the deal emerged in response to a credit crisis of early 1792, and effectively created a closed system, barring outside traders and increasing investor confidence.

Located in lower Manhattan, more specifically Wall Street, the Coffee House opened in 1794 and became an important venue in the city for the coming decades. It operated as a space for public meetings and as a merchants' exchange. As one contemporary writer reported, the venue was populated by 'underwriters, brokers, merchants, traders, and politicians', all of whom were engaged in 'selling, purchasing, trafficking, or insuring'. The site was alive with the activity of crowds 'bidding, or listening to the several auctioneers, and the streets outside jammed with carts, horses, and men'.[95] For a period, the Tontine Coffee House was the stock exchange of New York, with one contemporary account describing it as the place 'where all bargains are made'.[96] This remained the case until 1817, when the stockbrokers reorganised and moved to another premises on Wall Street.[97] The tontine which created the Coffee House was therefore significant for being an early step on the road towards the New York Stock Exchange.[98]

Some 200 miles or so north of New York, while the Coffee House was opening, a more contentious plan to fund the building of a grand block of townhouses via tontine was underway in Boston, Massachusetts. The design was the brainchild of American architect, Charles Bulfinch, who had recently returned from England full of inspiration, while the tontine was organised by a group of politicians and men from Boston's professional classes.[99] Over the next two years subscriptions were collected and the plan progressed under the control of the Boston Tontine Association. At this time all corporations required approval from the legislature, rather than simply just having to register that they existed. Unfortunately for the group, and as Kent McKeever has identified, there was a general antipathy in the Massachusetts legislature towards tontines at this time, and a charter was refused.[100] This appears to have been part of a wider culture war in which America's leaders, including John Hancock and Samuel Adams, expressed concerns, in the words of Heather Nathans, that 'the rising elite was overtaking the established structures of Boston society'.[101] Those behind the tontine were at the forefront of the new Boston elite, and their requests for incorporation were rejected multiple times.

As a result, the tontine money was converted into capital for the Union Bank, and the buildings, situated on the city's Franklin Place, were funded through the new institution. The building was completed in 1795, and within a few years all of the residences had been sold to some of Boston's most prominent business families.[102] Despite the building not being funded by tontine in the end, the name Tontine Crescent remained.[103]

Conclusion

Between 1750 and 1900, private tontines emerged to varying degrees across Britain, Europe, and North America. The groups which operated these creatively employed the tontine model to meet their communities' needs and demonstrate just how adaptable a financial instrument the scheme could be.

While mainland European territories, such as the Dutch Republic and German-speaking territories, appear to have viewed the tontine largely as an investment tool, in Britain, particularly Scotland and England, and to a lesser degree Ireland and Wales, it filled a vital role in financing civic improvements and urban development. Tontine-funded buildings like coffeehouses, theatres, and hotels became vital civic spaces for facilitating commerce, news-sharing, entertainment and public discourse. Additional applications of the tontine in Ireland, including covering private debts, providing working-class insurance benefits through mutual aid societies, and the peculiar temperance tontines incentivising sobriety, further demonstrate the flexibility of the scheme.

In the United States, tontines directed at building construction were less common. However, the New York Tontine Coffee House stands out as one of the most important buildings financed via tontine, serving as a forerunner to the New York Stock Exchange.

Ultimately, the diverse range of private tontine schemes catalogued in this chapter illustrates the importance of the tontine as a tool for raising capital and for catering to the economic and social needs of local communities between 1750 and 1900, and demonstrates the scheme's impact in shaping the built environment. Far from being disregarded as government-operated tontines declined in popularity, the tontine model proved malleable enough to be repurposed by private groups in creative ways. Its enduring legacy can still be seen today in the tontine-funded infrastructure, buildings and public spaces that remain part of our cities and towns.

Notes

1 D. Green, 'Tontines, Annuities and Civic Improvements in Georgian Britain', *Urban History*, Vol. 46 (2019), Appendix 1, pp.681–694.

2 D. Green, 'Tontines, Annuities and Civic Improvements in Georgian Britain', *Urban History*, Vol. 46 (2019), p.651; also see A. McDiarmid, 'The Development of Mutual Aid Tontines in Nineteenth Century Ireland', *Irish Economic and Social History* (forthcoming); and A. McDiarmid, '"Hardly a Kent Name Absent": Raising Capital in Scotland via Tontine, 1775–1850', *Journal of Scottish Historical Studies*, Vol. 43, No. 1 (2023), pp.31–53.

3 D. Green, 'Tontines, Annuities and Civic Improvements in Georgian Britain', *Urban History*, Vol. 46 (2019), Appendix 1, pp.649–694.

4 D. Clements, 'Invested in Identity: The Freemason's Tontine of 1775' (unpublished thesis), Institute of Historical Research, University of London (2018).

5 M. Milevsky, *King William's Tontine: Why the Retirement Annuity of the Future Should Resemble Its Past* (Cambridge: Cambridge University Press, 2015).

6 These have been identified through original research, as well as D. Green, 'Tontines, Annuities and Civic Improvements in Georgian Britain', *Urban History*, Vol. 46 (2019), Appendix 1, pp.681–694; and D. Clements, 'Invested in Identity: The Freemason's Tontine of 1775' (unpublished thesis), Institute of Historical Research, University of London (2018), Appendix 1, pp.129–131.

7 D. Green, 'Tontines, Annuities and Civic Improvements in Georgian Britain', *Urban History*, Vol. 46 (2019), Appendix 1, p.42; a second was operated in the town in 1791.

8 D. Green, 'Tontines, Annuities and Civic Improvements in Georgian Britain', *Urban History*, Vol. 46 (2019), Appendix 1, pp.684–694.

9 C.M. Norris, *The Financing of John Wesley's Methodism C.1740–1800* (Oxford: Oxford University Press, 2017), p.3; shares were priced at £30 each and 120 were sold.

10 See, D. Green, 'Tontines, Annuities and Civic Improvements in Georgian Britain', *Urban History*, Vol. 46 (2019), Appendix 1, pp.681–694; D. Clements, 'Invested in Identity: The Freemason's Tontine of 1775' (unpublished thesis), Institute of Historical Research, University of London (2018), Appendix 1, pp.129–131; and J.F. Nicholls and J. Taylor, *Bristol Past and Present: Civil History*, Vol. 1 (London: J.W. Arrowsmith, 1881), p.211.

11 D. Green, 'Tontines, Annuities and Civic Improvements in Georgian Britain', *Urban History*, Vol. 46 (2019), Appendix 1, p.658.

12 See, D. Green, 'Tontines, Annuities and Civic Improvements in Georgian Britain', *Urban History*, Vol. 46 (2019), Appendix 1, pp.681–694; D. Clements, 'Invested in Identity: The Freemason's Tontine of 1775' (unpublished thesis), Institute of Historical Research, University of London (2018), Appendix 1, pp.129–131; and S. Lewis (ed.), *A Topographical Dictionary of England* (London: S. Lewis, 1848), pp.440–444.

13 P.G.M. Dickson, *The Financial Revolution in England: A Study in the Development of Public Credit, 1688–1756* (London: Routledge, 1993), p.41; and *Some Considerations upon the Proposals approved of by the City of London for Subscriptions on Lives, Wherein are some Observations and Conjectures upon the East India Company and Banker*, in F. Hendriks, 'Notes on the Early History of Tontines', *The Assurance Magazine, and Journal of the Institute of Actuaries*, Vol. 10, No. 4 (1862), Appendix B, pp.213–219.

14 D. Green, 'Tontines, Annuities and Civic Improvements in Georgian Britain', *Urban History*, Vol. 46 (2019), Appendix 1, p.680 and Appendix 1, pp.681–694; *Monmouthshire Merlin*, February 12, 1870, p.8; and *Wrexham Guardian*, August 23, 1879, p.3.

15 D. Clements, 'Invested in Identity: The Freemason's Tontine of 1775' (unpublished thesis), Institute of Historical Research, University of London (2018), p.26.

16 *The Annual Register, or a View of the History, Politics, and Literature, for the Year 1773*, 3rd edn (London: J. Dodsley, 1780), p.129.

17 *The Annual Register, or a View of the History, Politics, and Literature, for the Year 1773*, 3rd edn (London: J. Dodsley, 1780).

18 D. Clements, 'Invested in Identity: The Freemason's Tontine of 1775' (unpublished thesis), Institute of Historical Research, University of London (2018), p.26.

19 Minute Book of the Commissioners of Richmond Bridge, 1773–1786, R.25.02-L624.2RAI, London Borough of Richmond Local Studies Library and Archive.

20 D. Clements, 'Invested in Identity: The Freemason's Tontine of 1775' (unpublished thesis), Institute of Historical Research, University of London (2018), p.26 and p.42.

21 D. Green, 'Tontines, Annuities and Civic Improvements in Georgian Britain', *Urban History*, Vol. 46 (2019), Appendix 1, p.692.

22 P.H. Lang, *Richmond upon Thames Through Time* (Stroud: Amberley, 2015), p.8.

23 It would not have been surprising if, in the years after the first English tontine in 1693, Scotland had followed suit and established its own scheme. There was after all, comparable development of financial ideas in both countries during the early 1690s, with a growth in joint-stock companies and the establishment of the Bank of England and the Bank of Scotland less than a year apart; see A. McDiarmid, *Credit, Currency and Capital: The Scottish Financial Revolution, 1690–1727* (Abingdon: Routledge, 2023), pp.9–12; and A. McDiarmid, 'The Equivalent Societies of Edinburgh and London, the Formation of the Royal Bank of Scotland, and the Nature of the Scottish Financial Revolution', *Journal of British Studies*, Vol. 60, No. 1 (2021), pp.88–114.

24 D. Watt, *The Price of Scotland: Darien, Union and the Wealth of Nations* (Edinburgh: Luath Press Limited, 2007), p.87.

25 Manufactories included a number of rope makers, cloth works, sugar refineries, soup makers, and coach builders also emerged between 1690 and 1695; see Gordon Marshall, 'Appendix: Manufacturing Enterprises in Scotland, 1560–1707', in *Presbyteries and Profits: Calvinism and the Development of Capitalism in Scotland, 1560–1707* (Edinburgh: Edinburgh University Press, 1992), 284–319 and A. McDiarmid, 'The Equivalent Societies of Edinburgh and London, the Formation of the Royal Bank of Scotland, and the Nature of the Scottish Financial Revolution', *Journal of British Studies*, Vol. 60, No. 1 (2021), p.90; for an overview of the Bank of Scotland see R. Saville, *Bank of Scotland: A History, 1695–1995* (Edinburgh: Edinburgh University Press, 1996), pp.22–25.

26 Even when a flurry of financial proposals were put to the Scottish Parliament in 1705, all of which were rejected, these did not include one for a tontine scheme; See A. McDiarmid, *Credit, Currency and Capital: The Scottish Financial Revolution, 1690–1727* (Abingdon: Routledge, 2023), pp.9–32; and A. McDiarmid, '"Bring Us Wealth, or KEEP IT among Us": The Financial Literature of the Edinburgh Pamphlet War of 1705, and the Capitalisation of the Scottish Economy', *The Scottish Historical Review*, Vol. 101, 2, No. 256 (August 2022), pp.179–209.

27 D.R. Weir, 'Tontines, Public Finance, and Revolution in France and England, 1688–1789', *The Journal of Economic History*, Vol. 49, No. 1 (1989), p.105.

28 A. McDiarmid, 'The Equivalent Societies of Edinburgh and London, the Formation of the Royal Bank of Scotland, and the Nature of the Scottish Financial Revolution', *Journal of British Studies*, Vol. 60, No. 1 (2021), pp.110–111.

29 A burgh was usually a town incorporated by royal charter and with a degree of autonomy.

30 B. Harris and C. McKean, *The Scottish Town in the Age of the Enlightenment, 1740–1820* (Edinburgh: Edinburgh University Press, 2014), pp.121, 123, 168, and 169.

31 For a detailed telling, see A. McDiarmid, '"Hardly a Kent Name Absent": Raising Capital in Scotland via Tontine, 1775–1850', *Journal of Scottish Historical Studies*, Vol. 43, No. 1 (2023), pp.31–53.

32 A. McDiarmid, '"Hardly a Kent Name Absent": Raising Capital in Scotland via Tontine, 1775–1850', *Journal of Scottish Historical Studies*, Vol. 43, No. 1 (2023), pp.31–53; A. McDiarmid, 'The Tontine and the Public Sphere: Ireland and Scotland Compared, 1772–1850', *The Geneva Risk and Insurance Review* (publication details forthcoming); D. Green, 'Tontines, Annuities and Civic Improvements in Georgian Britain', *Urban History*, Vol. 46 (2019), Appendix 1; and D. Clements, 'Invested in Identity: The Freemason's Tontine of 1775' (unpublished thesis), Institute of Historical Research, University of London (2018), Appendix 1.

33 D. Green, 'Tontines, Annuities and Civic Improvements in Georgian Britain', *Urban History*, Vol. 46 (2019), Appendix 1, p.688; and *The Scotsman,* Saturday November 20, 1841, p.1.

34 See A. McDiarmid, '"Hardly a Kent Name Absent": Raising Capital in Scotland via Tontine, 1775–1850', *Journal of Scottish Historical Studies*, Vol. 43, No. 1 (2023).
35 No author, 'Tontines and the Royal Bank', *Three Banks Review* (London, 1963), pp.28–36.
36 T. Meek, *The New Picture of Edinburgh, Being an Accurate Guide to the City & Environs; with Historical Descriptive Accounts of the Public Building, Offices, Institutions, Curiosities, Amusements, &c.* (Edinburgh: William Whyte and Co., 1814), p.258; and A. McDiarmid, '"Hardly a Kent Name Absent": Raising Capital in Scotland via Tontine, 1775–1850', *Journal of Scottish Historical Studies*, Vol. 43, No. 1 (2023), pp.36–37.
37 A. McDiarmid, '"Hardly a Kent Name Absent": Raising Capital in Scotland via Tontine, 1775–1850', *Journal of Scottish Historical Studies*, Vol. 43, No. 1 (2023), p.36.
38 A. McDiarmid, '"Hardly a Kent Name Absent": Raising Capital in Scotland via Tontine, 1775–1850', *Journal of Scottish Historical Studies*, Vol. 43, No. 1 (2023), pp.37–38.
39 When the *Glasgow Advertiser* (later the *Glasgow Herald* in January 1783, it did so in a format that echoed the information that had hitherto been available in the Tontine Buildings coffee-room. It provided advertisements for commercial endeavours, news from the London papers, and a 'tontine list' which provided information on the latest ships to arrive and depart from the Clyde port.
40 *Caledonian Mercury*, Monday, February 10, 1800, p.4; Saturday, March 8, 1800, p.4; Monday, September 22, 1800, p.4; Thursday, January 20, 1820, p.1; Thursday, November 13, 1800, p.3.
41 *The Welshman*, September 15, 1848, p.3.
42 *The Cambrian*, April 2, 1842, p.4.
43 *The Banker's Magazine; Journal of the Money Market and Railway Digest*, Vol. 9, January–December 1849 (London: Groombridge and Sons, 1849) pp.563–564.
44 *Inverness Courier*, January 24, 1850.
45 *The Banker's Magazine*, p.564.
46 A piece in the 7 August edition of *The London Mercantile Journal*, and which was widely reproduced in local press, outlines the issues with subscribers taking out their own life insurance policies: *London Mercantile Journal*, August 7, 1849; the piece was also reproduced in, among others; *Dundee Courier*, August 22, 1849; *Banker's Magazine*, August 1849; *Berrow's Worcester Journal*, August 23, 1849; *Stirling Observer*, August 23, 1849; *Elgin Courant, and Morayshire Advertiser*, August 24, 1849.
47 See, A. McDiarmid, 'The Development of Mutual Aid Tontines in Nineteenth Century Ireland', *Irish Economic and Social History* (forthcoming).
48 A. McDiarmid, 'The Tontine and the Public Sphere: Ireland and Scotland Compared, 1772–1850', *The Geneva Risk and Insurance Review* (publication details forthcoming); Royal Irish Academy, HT (Box) 470/21, *The Charter Party; or Articles of Agreement of the Tontine Buildings Company of the Town of Ennis; with a List of the Subscribers Names,* and also of Their Nominees (Ennis: M. Talbot, 1836).
49 *The Belfast Newsletter,* Tuesday, May 10, 1791, p.3; RIA, HP 1719/7, W.H. Carrol, *Proposed Prospectus for Forming a Tontine Company, for Building the New Intended Street, from Richmond Bridge to the Temple in the Queen's Inns between Henrietta Street and Constitution Hill, to Be Called, by Permission of the Most Noble the Marquis Wellesley, 'Great Wellesley Street'* (Dublin: W. Corbet, 1838).
50 RIA, SR 12 D 37, *Copy of the Deed and Charter, entered into by the Associated Society, to Raise a Fund for Erecting a Coffee-House and Other Buildings in the City of Cork; for the Government of the Said Society, and the Management and Disposal of the Funds Thereof, Dated 21st January, 1793* (Cork: Anthony Edwards, 1794), pp.4–5.

51 RIA, SR 12 D 37, *Copy of the Deed and Charter, entered into by the Associated Society, to Raise a Fund for Erecting a Coffee-House and Other Buildings in the City of Cork*, pp.3–4.

52 *New Cork Evening Post*, Thursday, November 28, 1793; *Freemans Journal*, Saturday, October 20, 1810, p.3; and *Cork Morning Intelligencer 1811–1812*, Tuesday, January 21, 1812, p.2.

53 K. Quinn, 'The Armagh Tontine Assembly Rooms', *History Armagh,* Vol. 4, No. 1 (Armagh, 2017), p.6.

54 S. Lewis, *A Topographical Dictionary of Ireland*, Vol. 1 (London: S. Lewis, 1837), p.68.

55 *Belfast Newsletter*, Friday, November 02, 1832, p.4; *Drogehda Argus and Leinster Journal 1835–1909*, Saturday, August 27, 1836, p.6; and *Belfast Newsletter*, Tuesday, September 01, 1840, p.4; E. Rogers, *A Record of the City of Armagh from the Earliest Period to the Present Time* (Armagh, 1861), pp.30–31; Quinn, 'The Armagh Tontine Assembly Rooms', p.5; and *Belfast Newsletter,* Tuesday, October 06, 1835, p.2.

56 *A List of the Nominees in the First Class of the Earl of Cork's Tontine*, (London: n.p., 1789)

57 T. Bartlett, 'The O'Haras of Annaghmore c. 1600—c. 1800: Survival and Revival', *Irish Economic and Social History*, Vol. 9 (1982), p.49; O'Hara sat in the Irish House from 1783 to 1800, and in the U.K. parliament from 1801–1822. His father had also been Irish MP (1761–1776), and had acted as head of a parliamentary committee tasked with reading over an amendment to the original tontine Act of 1773.

58 A Shields and V. Perry (eds), *O'Hara Papers*, Collection List 66, National Library of Ireland (Dublin, 2002), p.9.

59 A Shields and V. Perry (eds), *O'Hara Papers*, Collection List 66, National Library of Ireland (Dublin, 2002).

60 A Shields and V. Perry (eds), *O'Hara Papers*, Collection List 66, National Library of Ireland (Dublin, 2002), p.56.

61 *Report of Registrar of Friendly Societies in Ireland, for the Year Ending 31st December 1869*, in Accounts and Papers of the House of Commons (407) (London: n.p., 1870), pp.3–7.

62 *Report of Registrar of Friendly Societies in Ireland, for the Year Ending 31st December 1869*, in Accounts and Papers of the House of Commons (407) (London: n.p., 1870), 1869, pp.3–7. The figure will be higher than this as one society did not return its membership numbers.

63 J. Campbell, 'Tontine and Benefit Society Records in the National Archives and in the Registry of Friendly Societies', *Saothar*, Vol. 17 (1992), p.90.

64 J. Belchem, *Irish, Catholic and Scouse: The History of the Liverpool-Irish, 1800–1939* (Liverpool: Liverpool University Press, 2007), pp.7–8 and p.15.

65 A. McDiarmid, 'The Development of Mutual Aid Tontines in Nineteenth Century Ireland', *Irish Economic and Social History* (2024).

66 *Report of the Registrar of Friendly Societies in England for the Year Ending 31st December 1862*, in Account and Papers of the House of Commons (29), (London: n.p., 1863) pp.81–180; the one tontine which was not in Merseyside was the Manchester based St. Mary's Friendly Benefit Tontine.

67 *Report of the Registrar of Friendly Societies in England for the Year Ending 31st December 1863*, in Account and Papers of the House of Commons (32) (London: n.p., 1864), p.8 and pp.98–119.

68 *Registrar of Friendly Societies in England for the Year Ending 31st December 1866*, in Account and Papers of the House of Commons (39) (London, 1867), pp.98–211; and *Report of the Registrar of Friendly Societies in England for the Year Ending 31st December 1874,* in Account and Papers of the House of Commons (355) (London: n.p., 1875), pp.117–121.

69 *Report of Registrar of Friendly Societies in Ireland, 1877*, pp.292–299; T. Hunt, *Portlaw, County Waterford, 1825–1876: Portrait of an Industrial Village and Its Cotton Industry* (Dublin: Irish Academic Press, 2000), p.31; and A. McDiarmid, 'The Development of Mutual Aid Tontines in Nineteenth Century Ireland', *Irish Economic and Social History* (2024).

70 See, C. Kerrigan, 'The Social Impact of the Irish Temperance Movement, 1839–1845', *Irish Economic and Social History*, Vol. 14 (1987), pp.20–38; and J. Campbell, 'Tontine and Benefit Society Records in the National Archives and in the Registry of Friendly Societies', *Saothar*, Vol. 17 (1992), p.90.

71 *Monmouthshire Merlin*, February 17, 1838, p.1.

72 D. Green, 'Tontines, Annuities and Civic Improvements in Georgian Britain', *Urban History*, Vol. 46 (2019), Appendix 1, p.692; and *The Cambrian*, June 23, 1832, p.3; The Cambrian, October 5, 1805; In addition, there were two separate tontines in 1845 to fund the purchase of land. These were the Glamorganshire Tontine and the Monmouthshire Tontine, which raised £65,000 and £9,000 respectively; *The Cambrian*, October 17, 1845, p.1 and p.3.

73 D. Clements, 'Invested in Identity: The Freemason's Tontine of 1775' (unpublished thesis), Institute of Historical Research, University of London (2018), p.106; and E.J. Cleary, *The Building Society Movement* (London: Elek Books, 1965), pp.10–13.

74 *The Cambrian*, August 6, 1909, p.7.

75 *South Wales Daily News*, May 7, 1873, p.3; October 6, 1873, p.3: March 24, 1896, p.6; *South Wales Echo*, June 25, 1897, p.3.

76 L. Miskell, 'The Making of a New "Welsh Metropolis": Science, Leisure and Industry in Early Nineteenth-Century Swansea', *History*, Vol. 88, No. 1 (289) (January, 2003), p.40.

77 G. Bridges and S. Thomas, 'A Tontine, a Theatre, and It's Thespians: The Swansea Theatre, 1805–1899', *Journal of the Gower Society*, Vol. 45 (1994), p.38.

78 D. Green, 'Tontines, Annuities and Civic Improvements in Georgian Britain', *Urban History*, Vol. 46 (2019), Appendix 1, p.678.

79 D. Green, 'Tontines, Annuities and Civic Improvements in Georgian Britain', *Urban History*, Vol. 46 (2019), Appendix 1, p.678.

80 D. Green, 'Tontines, Annuities and Civic Improvements in Georgian Britain', *Urban History*, Vol. 46 (2019), Appendix 1, p.45.

81 D. Green, 'Tontines, Annuities and Civic Improvements in Georgian Britain', *Urban History*, Vol. 46 (2019), Appendix 1, p.46.

82 *The Cambrian News and Merionethshire Standard*, August 22, 1879, p.8.

83 *The Cambrian News and Merionethshire Standard*, December 5, 1873, p.10; *Wrexham Guardian*, September 2, 1876, p.5. and *Wrexham and Denbighshire Advertiser and Cheshire Shropshire and North Wales Register*, December 18, 1880, p.1; Three further schemes followed in the next decade. These were a tontine established by the union lodge of the Dolgellau chapter of the International Organisation of Good Templars, a fraternal orgnasation which promoted temperance (1873), and 'benefit and tontine society' (1876) and a sickness and burial tontine (1880), both in Wrexham.

84 *Wrexham and Denbighshire Advertiser and Cheshire Shropshire and North Wales Register*, December 24, 1892, p.4.

85 It should be noted that similar schemes to the mutual aid tontine did exist in Scotland in the form of 'dividing' Friendly Societies, but these were never referred to, or marketed, as tontines. See A. McDiarmid, 'The Tontine and the Public Sphere: Ireland and Scotland Compared, 1772–1850', *The Geneva Risk and Insurance Review* (publication details forthcoming).

86 J. Atack and L. Neal, *The Origins and Development of Financial Markets* (Cambridge: Cambridge University Press, 2009) pp.90–91; and K. McKeever, 'A Short

History of Tontines', *Fordham Journal of Corporate and Financial Law*, Vol. 15, Issue 42, (2009), p.493.

87 B. Sirks, 'Tontines in the Dutch Republic and the Early Kingdom (1670–1869)', in P. Hellwege (ed.), *The Past, Present, and Future of Tontines: A Seventeenth Century Financial Product and the Development of Life Insurance* (Berlin: Duncker & Humblot, 2018), pp.130–131.

88 B. Sirks, 'Tontines in the Dutch Republic and the Early Kingdom (1670–1869)', in P. Hellwege (ed.), *The Past, Present, and Future of Tontines: A Seventeenth Century Financial Product and the Development of Life Insurance* (Berlin: Duncker & Humblot, 2018), p.137.

89 P. Hellwege, *A History of Tontines in Germany: From a Multi-purpose Financial Product to a Single-purpose Pension Product* (Berlin: Duncker & Humblot, 2018), pp.26–27.

90 P. Hellwege, *A History of Tontines in Germany: From a Multi-purpose Financial Product to a Single-purpose Pension Product* (Berlin: Duncker & Humblot, 2018), p.27.

91 See, M. Fortunati, 'Tontines in Italy', in P. Hellwege (ed.), *The Past, Present, and Future of Tontines: A Seventeenth Century Financial Product and the Development of Life Insurance* (Berlin: Duncker & Humblot, 2018), pp.203–228; R. Illescas, 'Tontines in Spain', in P. Hellwege (ed.), *The Past, Present, and Future of Tontines: A Seventeenth Century Financial Product and the Development of Life Insurance* (Berlin: Duncker & Humblot, 2018), pp.229–237; M. Sunnqvist, 'Tontines in Scandinavia', in P. Hellwege (ed.), *The Past, Present, and Future of Tontines: A Seventeenth Century Financial Product and the Development of Life Insurance* (Berlin: Duncker & Humblot, 2018), pp.153–166; and B. Tokey, 'Tontines in Hungary', in P. Hellwege (ed.), *The Past, Present, and Future of Tontines: A Seventeenth Century Financial Product and the Development of Life Insurance* (Berlin: Duncker & Humblot, 2018), pp.289–296.

92 For examples of non-U.S. North American Tontines see K. McKeever, 'The Evolution of the Tontine in North America', in P. Hellwege (ed.), *The Past, Present, and Future of Tontines: A Seventeenth Century Financial Product and the Development of Life Insurance* (Berlin: Duncker & Humblot, 2018), pp.244–245.

93 K. McKeever, 'The Evolution of the Tontine in North America', in P. Hellwege (ed.), *The Past, Present, and Future of Tontines: A Seventeenth Century Financial Product and the Development of Life Insurance* (Berlin: Duncker & Humblot, 2018), pp.243–244; M.F. Sweetser (ed.), *New England; a Handbook for Travellers, A Guide to the Chief Cities and Popular Resorts of New England, and to Its Scenery and Historic Attractions; with the Western and Northern Borders from New York to Quebec* (Boston: Houghton, Osgood and Company, 1877), p.77; and 'An Act to Incorporate the Proprietors of the Brunswick Tontine Hotel', in *Special Laws of the State of Maine Passed by the Legislature, January 1828* (Augusta: n.p., 1828), pp.852–853; J. Lambert, *Travels through Canada, and the United States of North America, in the Years 1806, 1807, & 1808* (London: Baldwin, Cradock, and Joy, 1816), p.37.

94 This was through the sale of 203 shares priced at $200 each.

95 J. Lambert, *Travels through Canada, and the United States of North America, in the Years 1806, 1807, & 1808* (London: Baldwin, Cradock, and Joy, 1816), p.63.

96 H. Wansey, and D.J. Jeremy (ed.), *Henry Wansey and His American Journal*, 1794 (Philadelphia, 1970) p.75.

97 P. Eisenstadt, 'How the Buttonwood Tree Grew: The Making of a New York Stock Exchange Legend', *Prospects,* Vol. 19 (1994), p.75.

98 K. McKeever, 'A Short History of Tontines', *Fordham Journal of Corporate and Financial Law* (2009), p.500; when the original building was sold at auction in 1881, it realised $138,550, and provided each of the seven shareholders who were still active just shy of $20,000 each; see K. McKeever, 'The Evolution of the Tontine in North America', in P. Hellwege (ed.), *The Past, Present, and Future of Tontines: A Seventeenth Century Financial Product and the Development of Life Insurance* (Berlin: Duncker & Humblot, 2018), p.240.

99 P.S. Goodman, *The Garden Squares of Boston* (Lebanon, NH: University Press of New England, 2003), p.xi; and H.S. Nathans, *Early American Theatre from the Revolution to Thomas Jefferson: Into the Hands of the People* (Cambridge: Cambridge University Press, 2003), p.59.

100 K. McKeever, 'The Evolution of the Tontine in North America', in P. Hellwege (ed.), *The Past, Present, and Future of Tontines: A Seventeenth Century Financial Product and the Development of Life Insurance* (Berlin: Duncker & Humblot, 2018), p.241.

101 H.S. Nathans, *Early American Theatre from the Revolution to Thomas Jefferson: Into the Hands of the People* (Cambridge: Cambridge University Press, 2003), p.59.

102 P.S. Goodman, *The Garden Squares of Boston* (Lebanon, NH: University Press of New England, 2003), p.32.

103 For more information on successful and aborted private tontines in the United States see, K. McKeever, 'The Evolution of the Tontine in North America', in P. Hellwege (ed.), *The Past, Present, and Future of Tontines: A Seventeenth Century Financial Product and the Development of Life Insurance* (Berlin: Duncker & Humblot, 2018), pp.241–257; and K. McKeever, 'A Short History of Tontines', *Fordham Journal of Corporate and Financial Law* (2009), pp.500–501.

Bibliography

Primary Sources

An Act to Incorporate the Proprietors of the Brunswick Tontine Hotel', *Special Laws of the State of Maine Passed by the Legislature, January 1828* (Augusta: n.p., 1828), pp.852–853.

Belfast Newsletter, Friday, Tuesday, May 10, 1791; November 02, 1832; and Tuesday, October 06, 1835.

Caledonian Mercury, Monday, February 10, 1800; Saturday, March 8, 1800: Monday, September 22, 1800, Thursday, January 20, 1820; and Thursday, November 13, 1800.

Cambrian, October 5, 1805; June 3, 1832; April 2, 1842; October 17, 1845; August 6, 1909.

Cambrian News and Merionethshire Standard, August 22, 1879; December 5, 1873.

Carrol, *Proposed Prospectus for Forming a Tontine Company, for Building the New Intended Street, from Richmond Bridge to the Temple in the Queen's Inns between Henrietta Street and Constitution Hill, to Be Called, by Permission of the Most Noble the Marquis Wellesley, 'Great Wellesley Street'* (Dublin: W. Corbet, 1838), Royal Irish Acadamy, HP 1719/7.

Copy of the Deed and Charter, Entered into by the Associated Society, to Raise a Fund for Erecting a Coffee-House and Other Buildings in the City of Cork; for the Government of the Said Society, and the Management and Disposal of the Funds Thereof,

Dated 21st January, 1793 (Cork: Anthony Edwards, 1794), Royal Irish Acadamy, SR 12 D 37.

Cork Morning Intelligencer 1811–1812, Tuesday, January 21, 1812.

Drogehda Argus and Leinster Journal 1835–1909, Saturday, August 27, 1836.

Freemans Journal, Saturday, October 20, 1810.

Inverness Courier, January 24, 1850.

Lambert, J., *Travels through Canada, and the United States of North America, in the Years 1806, 1807, & 1808* (London: Baldwin, Cradock, and Joy, 1816).

'Minute Book of the Commissioners of Richmond Bridge, 1773–1786', R.25.02-L624.2RAI, London Borough of Richmond Local Studies Library and Archive.

Monmouthshire Merlin, February 17, 1838; February 12, 1870.

New Cork Evening Post, Thursday, November 28, 1793.

Registrar of Friendly Societies in England for the Year Ending 31st December 1866, in Account and Papers of the House of Commons, (39) (London: n.p., 1867), pp.98–211.

Report of the Registrar of Friendly Societies in England for the Year Ending 31st December 1862, in Account and Papers of the House of Commons, (29), (London: n.p., 1863)

Report of the Registrar of Friendly Societies in England for the Year Ending 31st December 1874, in Account and Papers of the House of Commons, (355) (London: n.p., 1875).

Report of Registrar of Friendly Societies in Ireland, for the Year Ending 31st December, 1869, in Accounts and Papers of the House of Commons (407) (London: n.p., 1870).

South Wales Daily News, May 7, 1873; October 6, 1873; March 24, 1896.

South Wales Echo, June 25, 1897.

Sporting Magazine, or Monthly Calendar of the Transactions of the Turf, the Chace, and Every Other Diversion Interesting to the Man of Pleasure, Enterprize and Spirit, October, (London: J. Wheels, 1797).

The Annual Register, or a View of the History, Politics, and Literature, for the Year 1773, 3rd edn (London: J. Dodsley, 1780).

The Banker's Magazine; Journal of the Money Market and Railway Digest, Vol. 9, January–December 1849 (London: Groombridge and Sons, 1849).

The Charter Party; or Articles of Agreement of the Tontine Buildings Company of the Town of Ennis; with a List of the Subscribers Names, and also of Their Nominees (Ennis: M. Talbot, 1836), Royal Irish Academy, HT (Box) 470/21.

The London Mercantile Journal, August 7, 1849.

The Scotsman, Saturday November 20, 1841.

The Welshman, September 15, 1848.

Wrexham and Denbighshire Advertiser and Cheshire Shropshire and North Wales Register, December 18, 1880; December 24, 1892.

Wrexham Guardian, September 2, 1876, August 23, 1879.

Books

Belchem, J., *Irish, Catholic and Scouse: The History of the Liverpool-Irish, 1800–1939* (Liverpool: Liverpool University Press, 2007).

Cleary, E.J., *The Building Society Movement* (London: Elek Books, 1965).

Clements, D., 'Invested in Identity: The Freemason's Tontine of 1775' (unpublished thesis), Institute of Historical Research, University of London (2018).

Dickson, P.G.M., *The Financial Revolution in England: A Study in the Development of Public Credit, 1688–1756* (London: Routledge, 1993).

Goodman, P.S., *The Garden Squares of Boston* (Lebanon: University Press of New England, NH, 2003).
Harris, B. and McKean, C., *The Scottish Town in the Age of the Enlightenment, 1740–1820*, pp.121, 123, 168, and 169 (Edinburgh: Edinburgh University Press, 2014).
Hellwege, P., *A History of Tontines in Germany: From a Multi-purpose Financial Product to a Single-purpose Pension Product* (Berlin: Duncker & Humblot, 2018).
Hunt, T., *Portlaw, County Waterford, 1825–1876: Portrait of an Industrial Village and its Cotton Industry* (Dublin: Irish Academic Press, 2000).
Lang, P.H., *Richmond upon Thames Through Time* (Stroud: Amberley, 2015).
Lewis, S. (ed.), *A Topographical Dictionary of England* (London: S. Lewis, 1848).
Marshall, G., *Presbyteries and Profits: Calvinism and the Development of Capitalism in Scotland, 1560–1707* (Edinburgh: Edinburgh University Press, 1992).
McDiarmid, A., *Credit, Currency and Capital: The Scottish Financial Revolution, 1690–1727* (Abingdon: Routledge, 2023).
Meek, T., *The New Picture of Edinburgh, Being an Accurate Guide to the City & Environs; with Historical Descriptive Accounts of the Public Building, Offices, Institutions, Curiosities, Amusements, &c.* (Edinburgh: William Whyte and Co., 1814).
Milevsky, M., *King William's Tontine: Why the Retirement Annuity of the Future Should Resemble Its Past* (Cambridge: Cambridge University Press, 2015).
Nathans, H.S., *Early American Theatre from the Revolution to Thomas Jefferson: Into the Hands of the People* (Cambridge: Cambridge University Press, 2003).
Nicholls J.F. and Taylor, J., *Bristol Past and Present: Civil History*, Vol. 1 (London: J.W. Arrowsmith, 1881).
Norris, C.M., *The Financing of John Wesley's Methodism C.1740–1800* (Oxford: Oxford University Press, 2017).
Rogers, E., *A Record of the City of Armagh from the Earliest Period to the Present Time* (Armagh, 1861).
Saville, R., *Bank of Scotland: A History, 1695–1995* (Edinburgh: Edinburgh University Press, 1996).
Shields, A. and Perry, V. (eds) *O'Hara Papers*, Collection List 66, National Library of Ireland (Dublin, 2002).
Sweetser, M.F. (ed.), *New England; a Handbook for Travellers, A Guide to the Chief Cities and Popular Resorts of New England, and to Its Scenery and Historic Attractions; with the Western and Northern Borders from New York to Quebec* (Boston: Houghton, Osgood and Company, 1877).
Watt, D., *The Price of Scotland: Darien, Union and the Wealth of Nations* (Edinburgh: Luath Press Limited, 2007).

Edited Collections and Journal Articles

Bartlett, T., 'The O'Haras of Annaghmore c. 1600—c. 1800: Survival and Revival', *Irish Economic and Social History*, Vol. 9 (1982), pp.34–52.
Bridges, G. and Thomas, S., 'A Tontine, a Theatre, and It's Thespians: The Swansea Theatre, 1805–1899', *Journal of the Gower Society*, Vol. 45 (1994), pp.38–47.
Campbell, J., 'Tontine and Benefit Society Records in the National Archives and in the Registry of Friendly Societies', *Saothar*, Vol. 17 (1992), pp.88–97.
Eisenstadt, P., 'How the Buttonwood Tree Grew: The Making of a New York Stock Exchange Legend', *Prospects*, Vol. 19 (1994), pp.75–98.

Fortunati, M. 'Tontines in Italy', in Hellwege, P. (ed.), *The Past, Present, and Future of Tontines: A Seventeenth Century Financial Product and the Development of Life Insurance* (Berlin: Duncker & Humblot, 2018), pp.203–228.

Green, D., 'Tontines, Annuities and Civic Improvements in Georgian Britain', *Urban History*, Vol. 46 (2019), pp.649–694.

Hendriks, F., 'Notes on the Early History of Tontines', *The Assurance Magazine, and Journal of the Institute of Actuaries*, Vol. 10, No. 4 (1862), pp.205–219.

Illescas, R., 'Tontines in Spain', in Hellwege, P. (ed.), *The Past, Present, and Future of Tontines: A Seventeenth Century Financial Product and the Development of Life Insurance* (Berlin: Duncker & Humblot, 2018), pp.229–237.

Jennings, R.M., Swanson, D.F. and Trout, A.P., 'Alexander Hamilton's Tontine Proposal', in *The William and Mary Quarterly*, Vol. 45, No. 1 (January, 1988), pp.107–115.

Kerrigan, C., 'The Social Impact of the Irish Temperance Movement, 1839–1845', *Irish Economic and Social History*, Vol. 14 (1987), pp.20–38.

McDiarmid, A., '"Bring Us Wealth, or Keep It among Us": The Financial Literature of the Edinburgh Pamphlet War of 1705, and the Capitalisation of the Scottish Economy', *The Scottish Historical Review*, Vol. CI, 2, No. 256 (August, 2022), pp.179–209.

McDiarmid, A., '"Hardly a Kent Name Absent": Raising Capital in Scotland via Tontine, 1775–1850', *Journal of Scottish Historical Studies*, Vol. 43, No. 1 (2023), pp.31–53.

McDiarmid, A., 'The Development of Mutual Aid Tontines in Nineteenth Century Ireland', *Irish Economic and Social History* (2024).

McDiarmid, A., 'The Equivalent Societies of Edinburgh and London, the Formation of the Royal Bank of Scotland, and the Nature of the Scottish Financial Revolution', *Journal of British Studies*, Vol. 60, No. 1 (2021), pp.88–114.

McDiarmid, A., 'The Tontine and the Public Sphere: Ireland and Scotland Compared, 1772–1850', *Genevan Risk and Insurance Review* (2024).

McKeever, K., 'A Short History of Tontines', *Fordham Journal of Corporate and Financial Law*, Vol. 15, Issue 42, (2009), pp.491–521.

McKeever, K., 'The Evolution of the Tontine in North America', in Hellwege, P. (ed.), *The Past, Present, and Future of Tontines: A Seventeenth Century Financial Product and the Development of Life Insurance* (Berlin: Duncker & Humblot, 2018), pp.244–245.

Miskell, L., 'The Making of a New "Welsh Metropolis": Science, Leisure and Industry in Early Nineteenth-Century Swansea', *History*, Vol. 88, No. 1 (289) (January, 2003), pp.32–52.

Quinn, K., 'The Armagh Tontine Assembly Rooms', *History Armagh*, Vol. 4, No. 1 (Armagh, 2017), pp.5–9.

Sirks, B., 'Tontines in the Dutch Republic and the Early Kingdom (1670–1869)', in Hellwege, P. (ed.), *The Past, Present, and Future of Tontines: A Seventeenth Century Financial Product and the Development of Life Insurance* (Berlin: Duncker & Humblot, 2018), pp.121–142.

Sunnqvist, M., 'Tontines in Scandinavia', in Hellwege, P. (ed.), *The Past, Present, and Future of Tontines: A Seventeenth Century Financial Product and the Development of Life Insurance* (Berlin: Duncker & Humblot, 2018), pp.153–166.

Tokey, B., 'Tontines in Hungary', in Hellwege, P. (ed.), *The Past, Present, and Future of Tontines: A Seventeenth Century Financial Product and the Development of Life Insurance* (Berlin: Duncker & Humblot, 2018), pp.289–296.

Weir, D.R., 'Tontines, Public Finance, and Revolution in France and England, 1688–1789', *The Journal of Economic History*, Vol. 49, No. 1 (1989), pp.95–126.

5 The Rise and Fall of Tontine Life Insurance in the United States, 1867–1906

Tontine life insurance policies provide an interesting intersection between the forms of tontine that have so far been the focus of this book and life insurance. Usually, a life insurance policy pays out when someone dies, but to benefit from tontine life insurance, one was required to survive. While these policies were not restricted to the United States, and also existed in Latin America, Europe, and Russia, it was American life insurance companies which led the way in their development.[1]

First emerging in 1867, tontine life insurance policies were developed by Henry B. Hyde as a means of allowing his relatively new Equitable Life Assurance Society, to compete with Frederick S. Winston's more established Mutual Life Insurance Company.[2] As the Equitable Life lacked the funds of its competitor, Hyde's new policies deferred dividends for a defined period in order to generate a financial surplus (assets minus any liabilities) and delay the payment of dividends, which were beginning to be paid more regularly than previously. In exchange, policyholders were promised larger future payouts; which did not always materialise.

What followed was a decades-long war between the two companies, carried out against the backdrop of a wider battle between those insurance companies which offered tontine policies and those which did not. Amidst the fighting, undertaken in the sector's press and in pamphlets and circulars, the sale of tontine policies grew rapidly during the second half of the nineteenth century, and by 1905 comprised two-thirds of all US life insurance policies.[3] It was not to last. A lack of transparency, accounting issues, and excessive corporate expenditures led to public scrutiny and investigations that signalled the demise of tontine life insurance by 1910.

This chapter provides a detailed look at the tontine life insurance trend that swept the United States, the corporate battles which fuelled it, and the final reckoning that recognised the tontine model's inherent conflicts when applied to life insurance products intended to provide security rather than speculative windfalls.

DOI: 10.4324/9781003491002-5

The Rise

The emergence of the first tontine life insurance policies in the United States were driven by competition and personal rivalry. Hyde was an ambitious young man, who, in 1852 at the age of 18, began working as a clerk for the New York-based Mutual Life Insurance Company; a corporation which had issued its first policy 9 years earlier, and which since then had consistently been an industry leader. For seven years Hyde rose through the company's ranks before announcing in 1859 that he was leaving to set up his own company.[4] After raising capital of $100,000, Hyde founded the Equitable Life Assurance Society in September of that year, renting an office in the same building and one floor above the Mutual Life offices.

The fledgling company was an early success, a fact that rankled which Hyde's ex-boss, Winston. In retaliation, and as he attempted to maintain his company's sales superiority, Winston used Mutual Life's size and established position in the market to put pressure on Hyde. Traditionally, those policies which paid dividends to policyholders had done so every five years.[5] In 1863, however, Winston changed this to every three years, a move which forced Equitable Life to do the same or risk losing out on business. While Hyde's company had been growing quickly, it did not have the same funds as the more established Mutual Life to pay the more regular dividends. In 1865, to cover the triennial dividend payments, Hyde was forced to empty the Equitable Life's surplus account, leaving the company in a vulnerable financial position. Winston was not finished, and sensing blood in the water he announced that Mutual Life would pay its first annual dividend in 1866. Hyde was forced to fashion some way of competing.

His solution was the tontine policy, also known as a 'deferred dividend' policy.[6] By postponing the payment of dividends for a specified tontine period (ranging from 5 to 20 years), the policy was designed to provide Equitable Life with a large surplus and pull the company back from the looming bankruptcy caused by the draining of the funds in 1865.[7] Hyde's innovative product fundamentally changed Equitable Life's competitive position. As these new policies offered future payments that couldn't be precisely compared to standard annual dividends, Equitable Life no longer needed to match the dividends paid by Mutual Life.[8]

The first tontine policy was issued in 1867, and worked by offering policy holders no initial dividends, no return premium (the amount of money returned to a policyholder if the cost of a policy is less than initially stated) nor any surrender value (the cash value of the policy minus any fees if the holder decided to surrender the policy) for the tontine period. Policyholders would always be paid a death benefit in the result of the nominated life dying, but no dividends would be paid during the tontine period. At the end of the agreed period, each surviving policyholder would then receive an annuity comprised of the following:

1 A yearly dividend
2 Interest due (the rate would be determined by the company)

3 A share of the surplus collected from policies which had terminated through death during the tontine period
4 A share in the surplus generated by those who had allowed their policies to lapse during the tontine period[9]

As was the case with the other types of tontines discussed in this book, these policies were designed to appeal to the gambling nature of policyholders. And while there were those in the industry that saw the scheme as 'life insurance cannibalism', the public enthusiastically bought into the concept of tontine life insurance.[10]

Hyde recognised that his new policy would allow policyholders to 'win' by living rather than dying; the inverse of traditional life insurance instruments. Advertisements for the scheme emphasised the sizeable dividends that policyholders could expect at the end of the tontine period, and company agents were induced to push the policies through generous commissions; Hyde himself also received a yearly 2.5 per cent cash bonus drawn from the overall surplus created by the policies.[11] Unsurprisingly, when other insurance companies saw the popularity of Equitable Life's new product, they followed suit. In 1870, Mutual Life began offering tontine policies, followed in 1871 by the New York Life Insurance Company.[12] These three companies between them possessed half the assets of all US life insurance companies and were responsible for the rapid growth of tontine life insurance.[13] Within a few years, most companies had adopted the tontine concept, with only three insurance firms of note, the Connecticut Mutual Life Insurance Company, the Provident Life and Trust Company of Philadelphia, and the Mutual Benefit Life Insurance Company of New Jersey, refusing to offer tontine policies.[14]

As documented in earlier chapters there was a strong connection between tontines and war, with European schemes often established to support the cost of military endeavours. In a manner, tontine life insurance carried on this tradition, as the Mutual Life and the Equitable Life companies engaged in a three decades long war to decide which company would reign supreme in the life insurance market. As a line in the sand, Mutual Life decided to stop issuing tontine policies in 1872. They had only been in this market for two years by this point and had had limited success, selling just 382 policies.[15] Winston issued a statement informing the public that the product had been withdrawn as trustees had decided they were 'wholly outside of the proper range of legitimate life insurance', and that rather than being a source of assistance, they were in fact failing 'the most needy'. There was also concern that the large surpluses being raised through the policies were providing companies with the 'strong temptation to wasteful expenditure, which, if indulged, may sooner or later bring disappointment even to survivors of those who play at tontine hazard'.[16] This last point very precisely foreshadowed what was to come.

While the Mutual Life and Equitable Life companies agreed on little, the tontine was the key point of division. Mutual Life mobilised its propaganda machine around the issue, and in 1872 began printing and distributing circulars which discredited the tontine and the Equitable Life company. A wider pamphlet war between the large number of companies which offered tontine policies and the smaller number of more traditional insurance companies which did not, also emerged at this time. Equitable Life took the brunt of the attack, and Hyde responded in kind in the insurance press, with the defamatory remarks between him and Winston continuing until the latter's death in 1885.[17]

In the meantime, Mutual Life, after renouncing the tontine, attempted to get the edge on its competition by reducing its premium rates by 25 per cent for new policyholders. Unsurprisingly, existing policyholders were enraged at the proposal, and the company was forced to row back on the plan. A similar situation occurred in 1878, when the Mutual Life board decided to offer new policyholders a rebate of up to 30 per cent on their first two premiums. Again, old customers rebelled, and the rebate plan was rescinded.[18] All this was happening as Mutual Life was determined not to return to tontine policies, and as Equitable Life was upping its commission rates and poaching its rival's best agents.

The sale of tontine policies continued at speed for Equitable Life and by 1884 it had passed Mutual Life in size, as did New York Life, which was also conducting tontine business. In 1885, Mutual Life's vice president Richard A. McCurdy and the company's agents successfully petitioned the board to end Winston's anti-tontine policy. Following the death of Winston in the same year, McCurdy was elected president of the company, and within three years, 99.5 per cent of Mutual Life's business was tontine-based.[19]

As war had been raging between the Mutual Life and Equitable Life companies, some significant changes had also occurred around the structure of tontine products. While the policies had been very popular, one source of criticism was the absence of any surrender value. This meant that policyholders lost everything if they surrendered the policy prior to the end of the tontine period. Many buyers had not realised this would be the case until they lapsed in payment or attempted to surrender the policy, and when some found out, they allowed the policy to lapse early, fearing they would eventually lose more later on.[20] In response, the semi-tontine policy was introduced. This mirrored the original tontine policy, paying out at the death of the nominated life, while still withholding the accumulated surplus, but with addition that any policyholder withdrawing from the policy would be entitled to a guaranteed surrender value. Following the change, the policies continued to sell well, with two-thirds of life insurance policies in the United States, a total of 9 million individual policies with a combined value of $6.2 billion, being tontine-based by 1905.[21]

The Fall

While tontine life insurance policies were incredibly successful, there had long been rumblings of discontent. When Equitable Life first promoted the scheme, the company had pushed the huge dividends that policyholders could expect to receive in the future. They failed to specify, however, exactly how much of a surplus would be raised through the policies and how much would be available for distribution at the time of their maturity. As we know, under the initial tontine policy, those policies which were terminated through death forfeited the accumulated surplus, while those which were surrendered were not entitled to any reserve value or any of the deferred dividends. It might therefore be assumed that these forfeited sums went into the accumulated surplus to be shared among surviving policyholders at the end of the tontine period. Equitable Life was, however, under no legal requirement to do this, and instead the actual final dividend amount was decided by the board of directors. The company was quite within its rights to balance its own requirements with the expectations of its policyholders. This allowed Equitable Life to direct some of the surplus raised into the business, by, for example, increasing commission and providing generous expense accounts for its agents in order to grow its share of the tontine market. A practice which eventually cut into customers' dividends.[22]

This kind of behaviour spread through the sector. Commission scales increased for agents and corporate salaries grew as life insurance companies fought for tontine business. It was common for prospective policyholders to be shown projections of returns which were hugely exaggerated. And when policyholders were provided with an annual statement, these were regularly falsified to support the overstated dividend estimates.[23] That this was able to happen was as a consequence of how tontine policies were organised. The absence of a system of annual accounting allowed underhand behaviour to remain undetected during the tontine period. It was only when payments became due, and policyholders received less than promised, that issues started to arise.

To cover the shortfall in payments to tontine customers, insurance companies were often forced to reduce the amount they were paying in annual dividends to non-tontine policyholders.[24] This was a move which only served to increase the grumblings coming from all policyholders about low payments. Tontine policyholders aired their grievances in news reports, pamphlets, and letters which detailed the disparity between the dividends received and what had been promised at the start.[25] Court cases between aggrieved tontine policyholders and insurance companies became commonplace.[26] And it became apparent to the wider public that something was not quite right in the life insurance industry.

The first investigation into the matter was conducted by the New York legislature in 1877. While the enquiry at this time was not focused on tontine insurance, and instead looked at wider mismanagement, fraud, and self-dealing within life insurance companies, the resultant report did find that accounting in relation to tontine policies was an issue.[27] Seven years later, in 1885, a more focused investigation into tontine insurance was undertaken by a committee appointed by the New York State Assembly. Investigators soon found they were hamstrung by a powerful insurance lobby which managed to restrict the investigation to just a few days. Limited by this, the committee focused its attentions on Equitable Life. In response, the company dodged requests to provide paperwork to aid the investigation.[28] Despite the recalcitrance of Equitable Life, the committee concluded that the:

> System or method practiced by the company in keeping accounts of ten-year policies, as well as fifteen-year and twenty-year policies, each in a class, instead of in yearly classes, makes it wholly impossible for any person other than a skilled actuary to determine the equitable rights of any one of the assured in any of the tontine classes[29]

This finding went to the core of the issues affecting tontine policies, accounting practices were simply not clear enough.

While the American requirements of the market appeared to be lax around the issue, companies began to get some pushback in foreign markets. An 1892 ruling in Prussia, where US life insurance companies were active, decreed that the companies must provide detailed accounting for their tontine policies. This led to Equitable Life withdrawing its business from the region, and the eruption of a trade war of sorts when Prussian companies were excluded from providing fire insurance in New York. Russia and Austria-Hungary also implemented more regulation around US tontine life insurance at this time.[30]

Despite the bad publicity, the life insurance sector adapted (for example, the implementation of the semi-tontine policy) and carried on with business. The real challenge came in 1905 when the New York legislature launched another investigation, this time focused on executive self-dealing and the complaints of disgruntled tontine policyholders.[31] Chaired by state senator, William W. Armstrong, with chief counsel, Charles Evans Hughes, the investigation invited 44 companies to participate.[32] The committee considered in depth, the advantages and disadvantages of the deferred dividend system, and focused on the practice of policy forfeiture for lapsed payments, along with the failure of companies to implement proper accounting practices for tontine policies.[33] After examining the evidence, the committee came to the same conclusion as the 1885 investigation, a lack of proper accounting was undermining the system.

The main recommendation of the Armstrong Committee was that 'companies should be compelled to exhibit the results of their management [of tontine policies] by annual accounting'. And if this was to be done, then there would be no reason why dividends should not also be paid annually, instead of being deferred. Companies retaliated by arguing that the practice of deferring dividends allowed them to protect themselves against market fluctuations and unexpected demands. The committee saw some merit in this but contended that the same could be achieved by establishing a contingency fund to protect policyholders, but which would only be made available if the company went into liquidation.[34] This would put an end to the large surpluses accumulated through tontine and semi-tontine policies which had proved too tempting for the insurance companies, creating the 'wasteful expenditure' that Winston had warned against back in 1870.[35]

In the two decades which preceded the Armstrong Committee, the assets of US life insurance companies had increased from $524 million to just short of $3 billion.[36] The amount of annual income against the amount companies were paying out also increased substantially, buoyed by the sale of tontine and semi-tontine policies, growing from $14 million to $230 million between 1865 and 1905.[37] In the aftermath of the committee's findings, things changed. In February 1906, the Armstrong Committee submitted its report to the New York legislature, and the result was eight new bills which passed into law in April of that year.[38] The sections of these new laws which affected the practice of tontine life insurance drew heavily on the committee's findings. Companies would be required to annually report on the accumulation of surplus linked to policies and provide details of its distribution. While this did not outlaw tontine policies, it made the model unworkable as dividends could no longer be deferred. The result was that tontine insurance was effectively abolished in the state of New York. Public hearings then followed in Wisconsin, New Jersey, and Massachusetts, which all followed New York's example. By 1910, tontine insurance was all but banned in most US states.[39]

Conclusion

The growth of US tontine life insurance across the second half of the nineteenth century, while dramatic, proved to be unsustainable in the long run. What began as a novel product fuelled by corporate rivalry ultimately collapsed under the weight of its own structural flaws and abuses by the early 1900s. At its core, the deferred dividend structure of tontine policies created problematic incentives and enabled a lack of transparency which fostered unethical corporate behaviour. With no requirement for annual accounting, insurance companies could exaggerate dividend projections, dip into policy surpluses for excessive expenditures, and leave policyholders in the dark until payouts came due. This speculative model was fundamentally misaligned with the purpose of life insurance to provide financial protection.

The Armstrong Committee's 1905 investigation shone a harsh light on these issues, forcing regulatory reforms that compelled annual accounting and effectively made tontine policies unviable. Within just a few years, tontine life insurance was practically outlawed across the US as the public and legislators recognised it as an unstable, gambling-like system rife with conflicts of interest.

The end of tontine life insurance was something of a death rattle for the tontine overall. While mutual aid tontines continued to operate in parts of Britain and Ireland during the early decades of the twentieth century, these were small local schemes in decline. Shutting down the highly lucrative market in tontine policies in the United States, therefore signalled the end of the tontine principle's use in any meaningful way in the western world for the remainder of the century.

Notes

1 As examples, for German and German speaking territories see, *A History of Tontines in Germany: From a Multi-purpose Financial Product to a Single-purpose Pension Product* (Berlin: Duncker & Humblot, 2018), pp.111–116, and pp.139–141; For Spain, see R. Illescas, 'Tontines in Spain', in P. Hellwege (ed.), *The Past, Present, and Future of Tontines: A Seventeenth Century Financial Product and the Development of Life Insurance* (Berlin: Duncker & Humblot, 2018), pp.230–233; For Latin America, see M. Nasser, 'Tontines in Latin America', in P. Hellwege (ed.), *The Past, Present, and Future of Tontines: A Seventeenth Century Financial Product and the Development of Life Insurance* (Berlin: Duncker & Humblot, 2018), pp 259–272; for Russia, see T. Korchagina, 'The Russian Experience with Tontine Insurance', in P. Hellwege (ed.), *The Past, Present, and Future of Tontines: A Seventeenth Century Financial Product and the Development of Life Insurance* (Berlin: Duncker & Humblot, 2018), pp.297–307.

2 These will be referred to as Equitable Life and Mutual Life.

3 R. Pearson, 'The Socio-Economic Setting for Developing Tontine from the 17th to the 19th Centuries', in P. Hellwege (ed.), *The Past, Present, and Future of Tontines: A Seventeenth Century Financial Product and the Development of Life Insurance* (Berlin: Duncker & Humblot, 2018), p.99.

4 R.W. Cooper, *An Historical Analysis of the Tontine Principle* (Philadelphia: University of Pennsylvania, 1972), p.10.

5 These were derived from excess funds generated by the company during the business year. Not all policies paid dividends.

6 K. McKeever, 'A Short History of Tontines', Fordham Journal of Corporate and Financial Law, Vol. 15, Issue 42, (2009), p.507; there are earlier examples of tontines and insurance intersecting. For example, the English Provident Life Assurance and Tontine Society (1856), and Tontine Fire Insurance Company (New York, 1855). Neither were successful, with the English Provident Life Assurance and Tontine Society ceasing business in 1857, and the Tontine Fire Insurance Company being mired in legal entanglements and never starting to trade. See, K. McKeever, 'The Evolution of the Tontine in North America', in P. Hellwege (ed.), The Past, Present, and Future of Tontines: A Seventeenth Century Financial Product and the Development of Life Insurance (Berlin: Duncker & Humblot, 2018), pp.247–248.

7 R.W. Cooper, *An Historical Analysis of the Tontine Principle* (Philadelphia: University of Pennsylvania, 1972), p.11.

8 R.W. Cooper, *An Historical Analysis of the Tontine Principle* (Philadelphia: University of Pennsylvania, 1972), p.11.

9 K. McKeever, 'The Evolution of the Tontine in North America', in P. Hellwege (ed.), *The Past, Present, and Future of Tontines: A Seventeenth Century Financial Product and the Development of Life Insurance* (Berlin: Duncker & Humblot, 2018), p.247.

10 R.W. Cooper, *An Historical Analysis of the Tontine Principle* (Philadelphia: University of Pennsylvania, 1972), p.13; this quote came from mathematician, Elizur Wright, often called the 'father of insurance regulation', who despite being against the principle, admitted that the mathematical principles were sound; see K.J. Meier, *The Political Economy of Regulation: The Case of Insurance* (New York: State University of New York Press, 1988), p.52.

11 R.W. Cooper, *An Historical Analysis of the Tontine Principle* (Philadelphia: University of Pennsylvania, 1972), p.13 and p.11.

12 R.W. Cooper, *An Historical Analysis of the Tontine Principle* (Philadelphia: University of Pennsylvania, 1972), p.14.

13 D.C. North, 'Life Insurance and Investment Banking at the Time of the Armstrong Investigation of 1905–1906', *The Journal of Economic History*, Vol. 14, No. 3 (Summer 1954), p.210.

14 R.W. Cooper, *An Historical Analysis of the Tontine Principle* (Philadelphia: University of Pennsylvania, 1972), p.14.

15 R.W. Cooper, *An Historical Analysis of the Tontine Principle* (Philadelphia: University of Pennsylvania, 1972), p.15.

16 Winston quoted in R.W. Cooper, *An Historical Analysis of the Tontine Principle* (Philadelphia: University of Pennsylvania, 1972), p.15.

17 K. McKeever, 'The Evolution of the Tontine in North America', in P. Hellwege (ed.), *The Past, Present, and Future of Tontines: A Seventeenth Century Financial Product and the Development of Life Insurance* (Berlin: Duncker & Humblot, 2018), p.249.

18 R.W. Cooper, *An Historical Analysis of the Tontine Principle* (Philadelphia: University of Pennsylvania, 1972), p.16.

19 R.W. Cooper, *An Historical Analysis of the Tontine Principle* (Philadelphia: University of Pennsylvania, 1972), pp.15–16.

20 R.W. Cooper, *An Historical Analysis of the Tontine Principle* (Philadelphia: University of Pennsylvania, 1972), p.17.

21 R. Pearson, 'The Socio-Economic Setting for Developing Tontine from the 17th to the 19th Centuries', in P. Hellwege (ed.), *The Past, Present, and Future of Tontines: A Seventeenth Century Financial Product and the Development of Life Insurance* (Berlin: Duncker & Humblot, 2018), p.99.

22 R.W. Cooper, *An Historical Analysis of the Tontine Principle* (Philadelphia: University of Pennsylvania, 1972), p.12.

23 R.W. Cooper, *An Historical Analysis of the Tontine Principle* (Philadelphia: University of Pennsylvania, 1972), p.21.

24 R.W. Cooper, *An Historical Analysis of the Tontine Principle* (Philadelphia: University of Pennsylvania, 1972), p.21.

25 K. McKeever, 'The Evolution of the Tontine in North America', in P. Hellwege (ed.), *The Past, Present, and Future of Tontines: A Seventeenth Century Financial Product and the Development of Life Insurance* (Berlin: Duncker & Humblot, 2018), p.249.

26 R.W. Cooper, *An Historical Analysis of the Tontine Principle* (Philadelphia: University of Pennsylvania, 1972), pp.37–42.

27 K. McKeever, 'The Evolution of the Tontine in North America', in P. Hellwege (ed.), *The Past, Present, and Future of Tontines: A Seventeenth Century Financial Product and the Development of Life Insurance* (Berlin: Duncker & Humblot, 2018), p.249.

28 K. McKeever, 'The Evolution of the Tontine in North America', in P. Hellwege (ed.), *The Past, Present, and Future of Tontines: A Seventeenth Century Financial Product and the Development of Life Insurance* (Berlin: Duncker & Humblot, 2018), p.249.

29 K. McKeever, 'The Evolution of the Tontine in North America', in P. Hellwege (ed.), *The Past, Present, and Future of Tontines: A Seventeenth Century Financial Product and the Development of Life Insurance* (Berlin: Duncker & Humblot, 2018), p.250.

30 K. McKeever, 'The Evolution of the Tontine in North America', in P. Hellwege (ed.), *The Past, Present, and Future of Tontines: A Seventeenth Century Financial Product and the Development of Life Insurance* (Berlin: Duncker & Humblot, 2018), p.251.
31 K. McKeever, 'The Evolution of the Tontine in North America', in P. Hellwege (ed.), *The Past, Present, and Future of Tontines: A Seventeenth Century Financial Product and the Development of Life Insurance* (Berlin: Duncker & Humblot, 2018), p.251.
32 R.W. Cooper, *An Historical Analysis of the Tontine Principle* (Philadelphia: University of Pennsylvania, 1972), p.43; and R.L. Ransom and R. Sutch, 'Tontine Insurance and the Armstrong Investigation: A Case of Stifled Innovation, 1868–1905', *The Journal of Economic History*, Vol. 47, No. 2, The Tasks of Economic History (June, 1987), pp.379–390.
33 R.W. Cooper, *An Historical Analysis of the Tontine Principle* (Philadelphia: University of Pennsylvania, 1972), pp.43–54; and K. McKeever, 'The Evolution of the Tontine in North America', in P. Hellwege (ed.), The Past, Present, and Future of Tontines: A Seventeenth Century Financial Product and the Development of Life Insurance (Berlin: Duncker & Humblot, 2018), p.251.
34 R.W. Cooper, *An Historical Analysis of the Tontine Principle* (Philadelphia: University of Pennsylvania, 1972), p.55.
35 R.W. Cooper, *An Historical Analysis of the Tontine Principle* (Philadelphia: University of Pennsylvania, 1972), p.15.
36 'The assets of all level-premium life insurance companies were $524,705,494 in 1885. By the end of 1905 they were $2,924,253,848', see D.C. North, 'Life Insurance and Investment Banking at the Time of the Armstrong Investigation of 1905–1906', *The Journal of Economic History*, Vol. 14, No. 3 (Summer 1954), p.210.
37 D.C. North, 'Life Insurance and Investment Banking at the Time of the Armstrong Investigation of 1905–1906', *The Journal of Economic History*, Vol. 14, No. 3 (Summer 1954), p.210.
38 R.W. Cooper, *An Historical Analysis of the Tontine Principle* (Philadelphia: University of Pennsylvania, 1972), p.56.
39 M. Milevsky, King William's Tontine: Why the Retirement Annuity of the Future Should Resemble Its Past (Cambridge: Cambridge University Press, 2015), p.122 and p.119.

Bibliography

Books

Cooper, R.W., *An Historical Analysis of the Tontine Principle* (Philadelphia: University of Pennsylvania, 1972).

Hellwege, P., *A History of Tontines in Germany: From a Multi-purpose Financial Product to a Single-purpose Pension Product* (Berlin: Duncker & Humblot, 2018).

Meier, K.J., *The Political Economy of Regulation: The Case of Insurance* (New York: State University of New York Press, 1988).

Milevsky, M., *King William's Tontine: Why the Retirement Annuity of the Future Should Resemble Its Past* (Cambridge: Cambridge University Press, 2015).

Edited Collections and Journal Articles

Illescas, R., 'Tontines in Spain', in Hellwege, P. (ed.), *The Past, Present, and Future of Tontines: A Seventeenth Century Financial Product and the Development of Life Insurance* (Berlin: Duncker & Humblot, 2018), pp.229–237.

Korchagina, T., 'The Russian Experience with Tontine Insurance', in Hellwege, P. (ed.), *The Past, Present, and Future of Tontines: A Seventeenth Century Financial Product and the Development of Life Insurance* (Berlin: Duncker & Humblot, 2018), pp.297–307.

McKeever, K., 'A Short History of Tontines', in *Fordham Journal of Corporate and Financial Law*, Vol. 15, Issue 42, (2009), pp.491–521.

McKeever, K., 'The Evolution of the Tontine in North America', in Hellwege, P. (ed.), *The Past, Present, and Future of Tontines: A Seventeenth Century Financial Product and the Development of Life Insurance* (Berlin: Duncker & Humblot, 2018), pp.244–245.

Nasser, M., 'Tontines in Latin America', in Hellwege, P. (ed.), *The Past, Present, and Future of Tontines: A Seventeenth Century Financial Product and the Development of Life Insurance* (Berlin: Duncker & Humblot, 2018), pp.259–272.

North, D.C., 'Life Insurance and Investment Banking at the Time of the Armstrong Investigation of 1905–1906', *The Journal of Economic History*, Vol. 14, No. 3 (Summer, 1954), pp.209–228.

Pearson, R., 'The Socio-Economic Setting for Developing Tontine from the 17th to the 19th Centuries', in Hellwege, P. (ed.), *The Past, Present, and Future of Tontines: A Seventeenth Century Financial Product and the Development of Life Insurance* (Berlin: Duncker & Humblot, 2018), pp.79–108.

Ransom, R.L. and Sutch, R., 'Tontine Insurance and the Armstrong Investigation: A Case of Stifled Innovation, 1868–1905', *The Journal of Economic History,* Vol. 47, No. 2, The Tasks of Economic History (June, 1987), pp.379–390.

6 The Long Shadow of the Tontine

In his lifetime, Lorenzo de Tonti was not a well-known Neapolitan banker. Nor was he the governor of the Italian city of Gaeta; he was, however, the governor of the town of Rossano for a short time, leaving office in acrimonious circumstances. He was not of noble descent. He was not the inventor of the tontine principle. He was not even Lorenzo de Tonti. Rather, the man who became Tonti, was a spy, a schemer, and a rapacious opportunist. In short, he was a chancer! He sought to turn any situation to his own benefit and appears to have been loyal only to himself. Yet, despite some significant character flaws, it was Tonti's development of a life annuity with benefit of survivorship in the 1650s that ignited interest in a scheme which would prove to be popular across Europe and North America over the centuries which followed. It was a project that Tonti returned to repeatedly, and one in which he appears to have had total belief in; or at least a belief that if anyone was going to make money from the tontine, it should be him. It is doubtful, however, that even Tonti could have foreseen the long shadow that 'his' financial instrument would cast across the globe.

As this book has demonstrated, the tontine principle was remarkably versatile, evolving from its earliest uses by local and national governments to its widespread adoption by private groups. This financial instrument served diverse purposes: funding wars, financing both private and public building projects, fueling investment schemes, and underpinning mutual aid societies and life insurance policies. Throughout these varied applications, the tontine remained a popular mechanism for raising capital and generating revenue, often with considerable effectiveness. Though, with many schemes failing to get off the ground, its success was not universal.

Beyond the financial organisation of the scheme, the projects to which the tontine was applied and the public interest around it represent some of the most fascinating elements of the story. From the late seventeenth century to the end of the eighteenth century, large-scale public tontines grabbed the national interest in the countries which operated them. They were debated in parliaments, reported on widely in the press, discussed in private, and encouraged the development of contemporary actuarial works.[1] When private

DOI: 10.4324/9781003491002-6

tontines then started to appear from the 1750s onwards, these were as investment schemes and more often as a means of raising capital for specific projects. While the former was the more prevalent on the European continent, the latter was the main form of tontine found in Britain and to a lesser extent the east coast of the United States.

When used to raise capital for projects, tontine funds were usually directed at covering the cost of civic improvements and urban development, and largely drew their organisation and investment from wealthier members of society, including the professional classes, local elites, and the mercantile community. The involvement of these groups determined the kind of projects funded via tontine, with investment funnelled into venues for conducting business, sharing news, socialising, and entertainment. Tontine-funded spaces subsequently became important local venues and contributed to the development of the public sphere in the locales where they were built. While tontines of this kind had ceased by the 1880s, for a period they proved to be a particularly favoured method of funding projects.

During the nineteenth century, alongside popular interest in private tontines for building projects and investments, innovative forms of tontine emerged. Most notable among these was the Irish mutual aid tontine, which marked a significant shift in the application of the tontine principle. These schemes stood apart from traditional tontines, being designed to support the working classes and poor in times of need. As such, they represented one of the most significant innovations to the concept since Tonti's original proposal. This form of tontine proved to be a crucial source of support in Ireland and in the Merseyside region of England, where migrant Irish communities established them.[2]

Other variations also appeared. temperance tontines, for instance, tied annuities to abstinence rather than longevity—a curious concept that merits further investigation. Perhaps most controversial was the American tontine life insurance, a volatile boom-and-bust scheme that merged the tontine principle with life insurance, and caused a scandal.

The Tontine in Culture and Literature

Given the widespread use of tontines, it is not surprising that the concept entered popular culture. As mentioned in this book's opening chapter, many readers may have preconceived notions about tontines and their operation due to literary representations of the scheme. Examples include novels by Robert Louis Stevenson and Agatha Christie, and even an episode of The Simpsons. Yet, these well-known instances only hint at the tontine's broader cultural impact, which extends far beyond these popular references.

Tontine references in fiction and popular culture were initially few and far between. The earliest appears to have been the 1708 play, *La Tontine*, by French playwright and novelist, Alain-René Lesage.[3] The work - a one act comedy, revolving around an avaricious doctor who hoped to marry his daughter off to an acquaintance as cheaply as possible by offering the prospective husband a dowry consisting of the returns gained from a tontine - was not, however, seen by an audience until 1732, and was only ever performed five times in public, before disappearing from the repertoire.[4] There was then an apparent absence of tontine references until 1777, when Anglo-Irish playwright, Richard Brinsley Sheriden, used it as a put-down in his comedy of manners, *The School for Scandal*.[5] At around this same time a tontine-based card game became popular among the French and British middle and upper classes; an occurrence which indicates a cultural awareness of the scheme.[6] During the nineteenth century the tontine appeared more regularly as a plot device in numerous novels, developing into somewhat of a trope in the next century, as novels and short stories were augmented by film and television.[7] Fictional renderings of the tontine have continued into the twenty-first century with several television shows and novels, a tontine-inspired board game, and a controversial American 'found footage' style movie of 2010.[8]

These representations have created a problematic narrative. At worst, they enforce the idea that underhand dealings and nefarious practices were common around the scheme. At best, they leave an uneasy feeling about benefiting from the demise of others. Depictions of the tontine in plays, novels, short stories, television, and film have done much to shape modern views of the scheme as a 'death lottery', in which participants, fueled by their own greed, are driven to commit fraud and even murder. This is a narrative which is refuted in part by historical scholarship. While there is recognition that instances of fraud linked to tontines certainly took place, there is no evidence of the scheme motivating anyone to commit murder.

The Tontine Today

While the word 'tontine' may not be one we use every day, we do still occasionally come across it, and indeed it is more common depending on where you are in the world. If you are in the UK or Ireland, it could be that there is a tontine building or a hotel in your town or city, such as in Glasgow, Cirencester, Limerick, Peebles, and Greenock to name just a few. In France, tontine clauses are used within mortgage agreements, which in the case of a death of one half of a couple who have purchased a property, the survivor is considered as always having been the sole owner/purchaser, thus avoiding the country's tricky inheritance laws. Financial schemes known as tontines are also active in African countries such as Nigeria, Ghana, Cameroon, and Zimbabwe.[9] In Cameroon, modern 'tontines' have moved online, with the development of mobile apps which allow investors to make and receive payments. These African schemes are, however, really savings and peer-to-peer lending tools, rather than traditional tontines, and do not have the benefit of survivorship. That they are widely known as tontines across the continent is nonetheless extraordinary.

New versions of the tontine are emerging in the modern financial landscape. Over the last decade, pension analysts and providers have shown renewed interest in the tontine principle and its potential applications in contemporary finance.[10] This revival extends to investment products as well. In September 2022, Canadian firm Guardian Capital LP launched the 'GuardPath™ Modern Tontine 2042 Trust', demonstrating the scheme's adaptability to current markets. While the rules governing this modern tontine are much stricter than in Tonti's day, the core premise remains: benefits accrue to survivors. Given this resurgence, it's likely that the tontine principle will become a more regular feature in modern financial instruments and pension products.

Conclusion

The concept of the tontine has demonstrated remarkable staying power and influence since the mid-seventeenth century. From funding wars and buildings, to entering popular culture through novels, plays and games, the tontine principle of last survivor taking all has proven to be an enduring financial and cultural concept. While its heyday as a revenue-raising vehicle for governments and as a private capital-raising tool has long since passed, the reemergence of the scheme in modern applications illustrates that the premise still has merit. The tontine's ability to adapt and be reinvented over multiple centuries is a testament to the enduring public fascination with games of chance combined with the opportunity, however small, of reaping a significant windfall.

Of course, for many of us, benefiting from the deaths of others remains unpalatable. Yet, as new versions of the tontine emerge, it's clear that Lorenzo de Tonti's curious financial instrument continues to cast a long shadow, one unlikely to fade anytime soon.

Notes

1 Examples of the latter E. Halley, 'An Estimate of the Degrees of the Mortality of Mankind, Drawn from Curious Tables of the Births and funerals at the City of Breslaw, with an Attempt to Ascertain the Price of Annuities upon Lives', in *Philosophical Transactions of the Royal Society*, Vol.17, Issue 196, (London, 1693), pp.596–610; A. de Moivre, *Annuities upon Lives: Or, the Valuation of Annuities upon Any Number of Lives; as also, of Reversions. To Which Is Added, an Appendix Concerning the Expectations of Life, and Probabilities of Survivorship* (London: W.P., 1725); and National Library of Ireland, P 32 (14), J.Y. Mathematician, *Tontine-Tables or, Calculations Respecting the Loan of £265,000; on Which Are to Be Granted Life Annuities of £6 Per cent with Benefit Survivorship* (Dublin: Thomas Watson, 1774).

2 A. McDiarmid, 'The Development of Mutual Aid Tontines in Nineteenth Century Ireland', *Irish Economic and Social History* (2024).

3 A.-R. Lesage, *La Tontine,* translated by F.J. Morlock (Chapel Hill: Project Gutenberg, 2004).

4 C. Bahier-porte, 'Dans l'atelier de Lesage : l'histoire de La Tontine, des manuscrits au livre (1708-1739)', in Revue d'histoire littéraire de la France 2011/4 (Vol. 111), p.838

5 R.B. Sheriden, *The School for* Scandal, H.H. Webster (ed.) (Boston: Houghton Mifflin Company, 1917), p.26; Originally written in 1777: When a group are rather cattily discussing the character of Charles Surface, it is remarked 'l hear he pays as many annuities as the lrish Tontine'.

6 *The Sporting Magazine, or Monthly Calendar of the Transactions of the Turf, the Chace, and Every Other Diversion Interesting to the Man of Pleasure, Enterprize and Spirit*, October, (London: J. Wheels, 1797).

7 This list is by no means exhaustive; Novels include, H.H. Smart, *The Great Tontine* (London: Ward, Lock, and Co., 1881); R.L. Stevenson and L. Osbourne, *The Wrong Box* (LondonLongmans, Green & Co., 1889); R.M. Gilchrist, *The Secret Tontine* (London: John Long, 1912); T.B. Constain, *The Tontine*, Vol. 1–2 (New York: Doubleday and Company, 1955); A. Christie, *4.50 from Paddington* (London: Collins Crime Club, 1957); P.G. Wodehouse, *Something Fishy* (London: Herbert Jenkins, 1957); Television shows include 'The Wild Wild West', 'The Night of the Tottering Tontine', Season 2, Episode 16, 1966; 'M*A*S*H', 'Old Soldiers', Season 8, Episode 18, 1980; and 'The Simpsons', 'Raging Abe Simpson and His Grumbling Grandson in "The Curse of the Flying Hellfish"', Season 7, Episode 22, 1996.

8 These include, 'Tomcats', Revolution Studios (2001); 'Tontine', E. Sandz (2010); 'Archer', 'Double Deuce', Season 2, Episode 5 (2011); 'Dead Last' (Boardgame), Smirk and Dagger Games (2016); and P.J. Fitzimmons, *The Tale of the Tenpenny Tontine* (London: Phillip Fitzsimmons, 2021).

9 S. Mancuso, 'Tontines and other Forms of Rotating Credit Associations in Africa', in P. Hellwege (ed.), *The Past, Present, and Future of Tontines: A Seventeenth Century Financial Product and the Development of Life Insurance* (Berlin: Duncker & Humblot, 2018), pp.343–366.

10 As examples see, M.A. Milevsky and T.S. Salisbury, 'Optimal Retirement Tontines for the 21st Century: With Reference to Mortality Derivatives in 1693', SSRN Open Access (2013); J.B. Forman and M.J. Sabin, 'Tontine Pensions', *University of Pennsylvania Law Review*, Vol. 163, Issue 3, (2015), available at https://papers.ssrn.com/sol3/papers.cfm?abstract_id=2271259, pp.755–831; Forman and Sabin, 'The Analytics of a Single-Period Tontine' (2016), SSRN Open Access; M. Milevsky, *King William's Tontine: Why the Retirement Annuity of the Future Should Resemble Its Past* (Cambridge: Cambridge University Press, 2015); T. Bernhardt and C. Donnelly, 'Modern Tontine with Bequest: Innovation in Pooled Annuity Products', *Insurance: Mathematics and Economics*, Vol. 86 (May, 2019), pp.168–188.

Bibliography

Primary Sources

Christie, A., *4.50 from Paddington* (London: Collins Crime Club, 1957).

de Moivre, A., *Annuities upon Lives: Or, the Valuation of Annuities upon Any Number of Lives; as also, of Reversions. To Which Is Added, an Appendix Concerning the Expectations of Life, and Probabilities of Survivorship* (Londo: W.P., 1725)

Constain, T.B., *The Tontine*, Vol. 1–2 (New York: Doubleday and Company, 1955).

Fitzimmons, P.J., *The Tale of the Tenpenny Tontine* (London: Phillip Fitzsimmons, 2021).

Gilchrist, R.M., *The Secret Tontine* (London: John Long, 1912).

Guo, J., 'It's Sleazy, It's Totally Illegal, and Yet It Could Become the Future of Retirement', *Washington Post* (September 28, 2015).

Halley, E., 'An Estimate of the Degrees of the Mortality of Mankind, Drawn from Curious Tables of the Births and funerals at the City of Breslaw, with an Attempt to Ascertain the Price of Annuities upon Lives', in *Philosophical Transactions of the Royal Society*, Vol.17, Issue 196, (London, 1693), pp.596–610

Lesage, A.-R., *La Tontine*, translated by F.J. Morlock (Chapel Hill: Project Gutenberg, 2004).

Mathematician, J.Y. *Tontine-Tables or, Calculations Respecting the Loan of £265,000; on Which Are to Be Granted Life Annuities of £6 Per cent with Benefit Survivorship* (Dublin: Thomas Watson, 1774). NLI P 32 (14),

Sheriden, R.B., *The School for Scandal*, H.H. Webster (ed.) (Boston: Houghton Mifflin Company, 1917).

Smart, H.H., *The Great Tontine* (London: Ward, Lock, and Co., 1881).

Sporting Magazine, or Monthly Calendar of the Transactions of the Turf, the Chace, and Every Other Diversion Interesting to the Man of Pleasure, Enterprize and Spirit, October, (London: J. Wheels, 1797).

Stevenson, R.L. and Osbourne, L., *The Wrong Box* (LondonLongmans, Green & Co., 1889).

Wodehouse, P.G., *Something Fishy* (London: Herbert Jenkins, 1957).

Books

Milevsky, M., *King William's Tontine: Why the Retirement Annuity of the Future Should Resemble Its Past* (Cambridge: Cambridge University Press, 2015).

Edited Collections and Journal Articles

Bahier-porte, C., 'Dans l'atelier de Lesage : l'histoire de La Tontine, des manuscrits au livre (1708-1739)', in Revue d'histoire littéraire de la France 2011/4 (Vol. 111), pp. 837–850

Bernhardt, T. and Donnelly, C., 'Modern Tontine with Bequest: Innovation in Pooled Annuity Products', *Insurance: Mathematics and Economics*, Vol. 86 (May, 2019), pp.168–188.

Forman, J.B. and Sabin, M.J., 'Tontine Pensions', *University of Pennsylvania Law Review*, Vol. 163, Issue 3, (2015), pp.755–831.

Forman, J.B. and Sabin, M.J., 'The Analytics of a Single-Period Tontine', *SSRN Open Access* (2016).

Gallais-Hamonno, G. and Rietsch, O., 'Financial Engineering in the 17th and 18th Centuries', in Hellwege, P. (ed.), *The Past, Present, and Future of Tontines: A Seventeenth Century Financial Product and the Development of Life Insurance* (Berlin: Duncker & Humblot, 2018), pp.49–78.

Mancuso, S., 'Tontines and Other Forms of Rotating Credit Associations in Africa', in Hellwege, P. (ed.), *The Past, Present, and Future of Tontines: A Seventeenth Century Financial Product and the Development of Life Insurance* (Berlin: Duncker & Humblot, 2018), pp.343–366.

McDiarmid, A., 'The Development of Mutual Aid Tontines in Nineteenth Century Ireland', *Irish Economic and Social History*, Open Access (2024).

Milevsky, M.A. and Salisbury, T.S., 'Optimal Retirement Tontines for the 21st Century: With Reference to Mortality Derivatives in 1693', SSRN Open Access (2013).

Weir, D.R., 'Public Finance, and Revolution in France and England, 1688–1789', *The Journal of Economic History*, Vol. 49, No. 1 (March, 1989), pp.95–124.

Television Shows and Movies

'Archer', 'Double Deuce', Season 2, Episode 5 (2011).

'M*A*S*H', 'Old Soldiers', Season 8, Episode 18 (1980).

'The Simpsons', 'Raging Abe Simpson and His Grumbling Grandson in "The Curse of the Flying Hellfish"', Season 7, Episode 22 (1996).

'The Wild Wild West', 'The Night of the Tottering Tontine', Season 2, Episode 16 (1966).

'Tomcats', Revolution Studios (2001).

'Tontine', E. Sandz (2010).

Index

Printed and bound by CPI Group (UK) Ltd, Croydon, CR0 4YY
08/10/2024
01042477-0003